Praise

"Maddie Lock's memoir quietly opens some of the closed doors of family life as it struggles to return to normalcy in post-World War II Germany—and ventures further. The war and post-war years gave birth to hundreds of thousands of children born out of wedlock internationally. In Germany, they were encouraged and sanctioned under the Lebensborn project to expand Aryan populations, but worldwide they were mostly the result of the transient and anonymous nature of war. In confronting both of those forms of illegitimacy in her family's and her own life, Lock seeks a resolution to the questions of Who am I? and Where is my home? that always underlie the lives of many of the children of any war."

Chris Dickon, co-author of
Dutch Children of African American Liberators

"It takes immense courage to unearth deeply buried family truths—especially those hidden for good reason. In *Illegitimate*, Maddie Lock undertakes a brave and deeply personal journey to uncover the identity of the father she never knew. Her search for answers to questions of identity, abandonment, and belonging becomes even more complex when entwined with the chilling legacy of Nazi Germany. Lock's story is not hers alone. Several of her mother's siblings were born under the Lebensborn programme, a sinister initiative designed to promote the Aryan ideal. This dark historical backdrop casts a long shadow over the family's history, shaping lives in ways both overt and silent. With raw honesty and emotional depth, Lock reminds us that even when memories fail, the heart remembers."

Angela Findlay, author of *In My Grandfather's Shadow: A story of war, trauma and the legacy of silence*

"This memoir is deftly rendered and illustrates the value of exploring uncomfortable and painful truths. Lock's quest for connection and rootedness takes us from disillusionment to a greater promise, uncovering the beauty and potential of human resilience."

Jen Knox, author of *We Arrive Uninvited and Radicals*

"A moving and beautifully-written memoir of lives shaped and shattered by the Nazi creed—and caught in the trailing tendrils of Hitler's obsession with blood and an Aryan future."

Tim Tate, investigative journalist, filmmaker, co-author of *Hitler's Forgotten Children*

"After the revelation of a long-held family secret, Maddie Lock embarks on a lengthy journey to excavate the truth about her family and build a relationship with the Papa she never knew. As she traverses two worlds, Germany, the land of her birth, and the United States, her home—an outlander in each—she discovers how generations of her family were shaped by a diabolical Nazi program. *Illegitimate* is, ultimately, a deeply compelling story of love, forgiveness, and redemption."

B.K. Jackson, founder of *Severance Magazine* and editor of the forthcoming anthology *Relative Strangers*

"*Illegitimate* is the heartbreaking story of a woman who wants to know her origins and discovers they lead straight to the heart of darkness of the 20th century: the Nazis' Lebensborn project to create the perfect Aryan race. Her story is also proof of how fearless exploration of history can be rewarding, as she connects and solidifies her family ties."

Thomas Geiger, editor, publisher, magazine editor, and former curator and moderator at Literary Colloquium Berlin

"A true exploration of the past and of self, Lock digs at scars of self, family, and history, taking the reader on a personal journey that does not flinch in the face of what *Illegitimate* finds. Lock digests her family history and intimate tie to what history does not want to admit to in this stunning, eye-opening, and revelatory—to the author and to the reader—memoir."

Kase Johnstun, MA, MFA, author of *Cast Away*, editor of *Label Me Latina/o Literary Journal*

About the Author

German-born and adopted by an American Army officer, Maddie Lock graduated with a BA in English Lit from the University of South Florida. She began a freelance journalism career before sidetracking into the corporate business world. After founding and selling a successful multi-million dollar enterprise, she returned to her first love of writing. Maddie is the author of two children's books, including the RPLA award-winning *Ethel the Backyard Dog*. Her essays have been published in various journals and anthologies, including the *Unleash Conversations* anthology in which her essay "The Stranger" won Editor's Pick. On a trip to her homeland in 2013, Maddie discovered a long-held family secret with tentacles reaching back to Hitler, which began a journey of research, revelation, and redemption.

www.maddielock.com

MADDIE
LOCK

ILLEGITIMATE

www.vineleavespress.com

ILLEGITIMATE: A Daughter's Search for Truth in the Shadow of Lebensborn

Print Edition
ISBN: 978-3-98832-222-7
Published by Vine Leaves Press 2026

Cover design by Jessica Bell
Interior design by Amie McCracken

To my dear Papa, Walter Harth
1926–2024

And to my indomitable Aunt Sieglinde

My mother recalled fondly the nasturtiums that grew abundantly in Oma's garden. Not only are they lovely in bloom but can also be a source of food. The leaves, flowers, and immature seed pods offer a spicy, peppery flavor, a welcome addition to the sparse and often flavorless food of WWII. With its entangled stems that give way to beautiful blooms, the nasturtium represents the interconnectedness of family, along with the growth and flexibility we need for acceptance and support of each other.

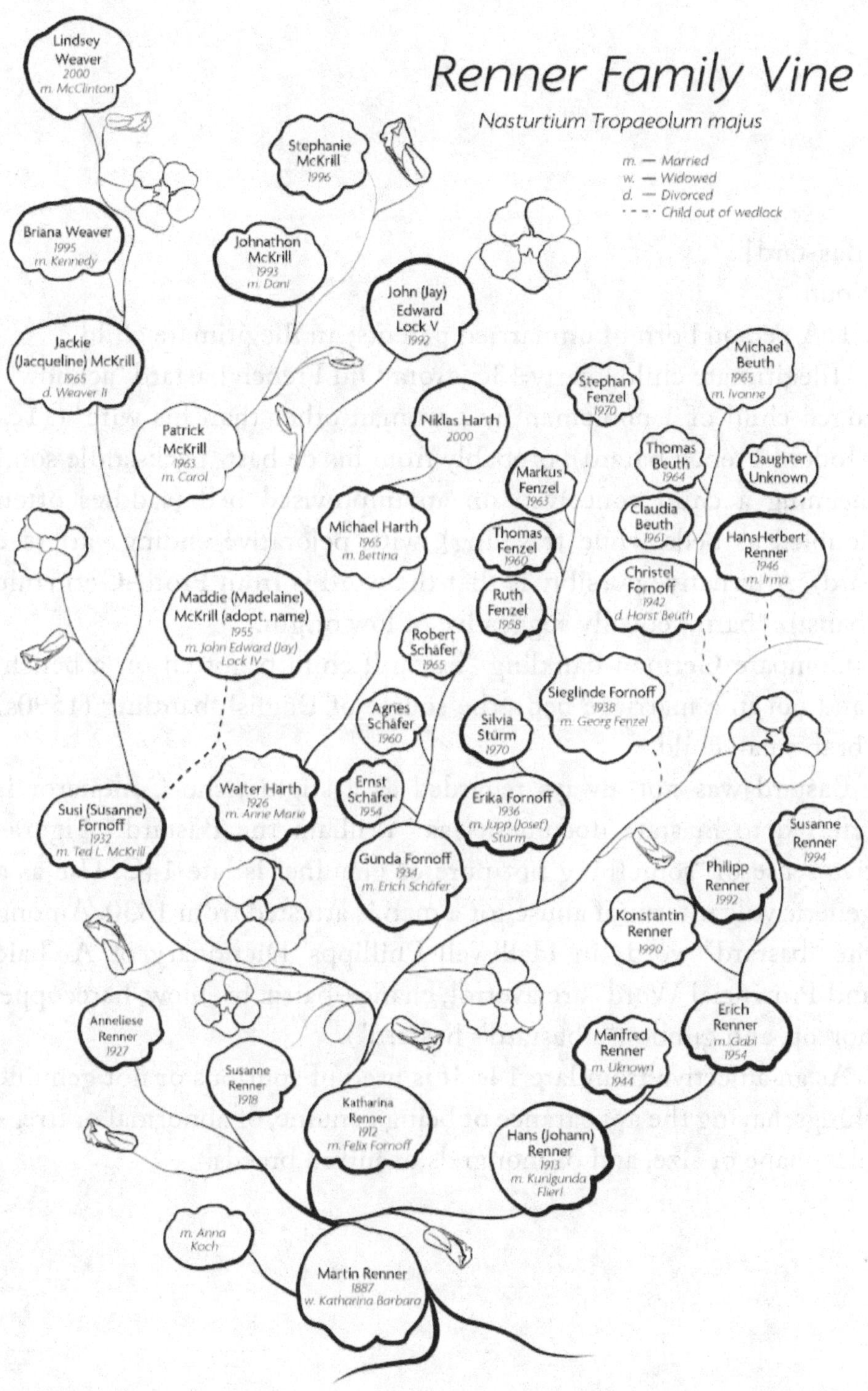
Renner Family Vine
Nasturtium Tropaeolum majus
m. — Married
w. — Widowed
d. — Divorced
Child out of wedlock
Lindsey Weaver 2000 m. McClinton
Stephanie McKrill 1996
Briana Weaver 1995 m. Kennedy
Johnathon McKrill 1993 m. Dani
John (Jay) Edward Lock V 1992
Jackie (Jacqueline) McKrill 1965 d. Weaver II
Michael Beuth 1965 m. Ivonne
Stephan Fenzel 1970
Niklas Harth 2000
Patrick McKrill 1963 m. Carol
Thomas Beuth 1964
Daughter Unknown
Markus Fenzel 1963
Claudia Beuth 1961
Michael Harth 1965 m. Bettina
Thomas Fenzel 1960
HansHerbert Renner 1946 m. Irma
Christel Fornoff 1942 d. Horst Beuth
Ruth Fenzel 1958
Maddie (Madelaine) McKrill (adopt. name) 1955 m. John Edward (Jay) Lock IV
Robert Schäfer 1965
Sieglinde Fornoff 1938 m. Georg Fenzel
Agnes Schäfer 1960
Silvia Stürm 1970
Walter Harth 1926 m. Anne Marie
Ernst Schäfer 1954
Erika Fornoff 1936 m. Jupp (Josef) Stürm
Susi (Susanne) Fornoff 1932 m. Ted L. McKrill
Gunda Fornoff 1934 m. Erich Schäfer
Susanne Renner 1994
Philipp Renner 1992
Konstantin Renner 1990
Anneliese Renner 1927
Erich Renner m. Gabi 1954
Manfred Renner m. Uknown 1944
Susanne Renner 1918
Katharina Renner 1912 m. Felix Fornoff
Hans (Johann) Renner 1913 m. Kunigunda Flierl
m. Anna Koch
Martin Renner 1887 w. Katharina Barbara

[Bas-tard]
Noun

1. A person born of unmarried parents; an illegitimate child.

"Illegitimate child," early 13c., from Old French bastard "acknowledged child of a nobleman by a woman other than his wife" (11c., Modern French bâtard), probably from fils de bast "packsaddle son," meaning a child conceived on an improvised bed (saddles often doubled as beds while traveling), with pejorative ending -art (see -ard). Alternative possibly is that the word is from Proto-Germanic *banstiz "barn," equally suggestive of low origin.

Compare German bänkling "bastard; child begotten on a bench" (and not in a marriage bed), the source of English bantling (1590s) "brat, small child."

Bastard was not always regarded as a stigma; the Conqueror is referred to in state documents as "William the Bastard." Figurative sense of "something not pure or genuine" is late 14C. Use as a generic vulgar term of abuse for a man is attested from 1830. Among the "bastard" words in Halliwell-Phillipps' Dictionary of Archaic and Provincial Words are avetrol, chance-bairn, by-blow, harecoppe, horcop, and gimbo ("a bastard's bastard").

As an adjective from late 14c. it is used of spurious or not genuine things, having the appearance of being genuine, of abnormal or irregular shape or size, and of mongrels or mixed breeds.

Author's Note

The story that unfolds in this book is told as truthfully as possible, based on my notes, recollection, and research. Many conversations have been translated from German. Any errors are my responsibility.

The Revelation
A Prologue

Sulzbach
May 2013

Here we were, as memory serves, in a small café on a cobblestone street of the historic town in Bavaria that holds the ghosts and shadows of my maternal family. A group of us were enjoying *gemütlichkeit*, that wonderful German tradition of eating, drinking, and laughing for no good reason. This was the first day of a much-anticipated road trip through Austria, Italy, and Switzerland with my cousin Michael who, at forty-eight, was ten years younger than me. We had stopped here to visit our seventy-five-year-old Aunt Sieglinde. Her oldest son, Thomas, had driven from Munich to join us.

My lovely blonde-haired, blue-eyed aunt took a delicate sip of wine, a deep breath, and then changed our family history forever.

"I found my father."

What?

I glanced at my cousin Michael sitting next to me. He too had a question mark on his face. My grandpa Felix, Sieglinde's supposed father and the one we knew as our grandpa for all our lives, had been a lance-corporal in Hitler's *Wehrmacht* and died on the front in 1944. We never knew where he was buried; perhaps she had found out where his grave was?

"Felix was not my father. In fact, he only fathered the first three girls. The rest of us all had different fathers. My father was a doctor who worked in prosthetics. I found him, but I never got to meet him before he died."

The table was silent as we continued to stare at Sieglinde. She took a moment to compose herself. And in a voice that held both doubt and determination, she told us.

"I was a baby made for Hitler."

My scrambled thoughts tried to make sense of her words, as they ricocheted around in my brain. *A baby made for Hitler?* I knew my maternal grandmother, Sieglinde's mother—Oma Katharina—as the loving woman who took me in as an infant while my single mother traveled the world as part of a dance troupe. Not someone who was involved in Nazi eugenic programs to promote the Aryan race.

We shifted in our seats, glancing at one another. *Now what?* Sieglinde's face told us she had said too much. The setting was wrong; the mood had turned. I can't remember what happened next. The evening turned surreal. It wasn't long before Sieglinde bade us a brisk goodnight, picked up her purse, and stepped through the door out onto the cobblestone streets for the short walk home. The clinking of silverware from other tables suddenly sounded out of place.

•

We left the café in silence, absorbing the impact on our family. All the genetics we would never know. Questions pelted me. Who was this doctor? How did my grandmother meet him? Was she approached; did she volunteer? Why would she risk her family to do this? What about Michael's mother, Christel? According to Sieglinde, she also had an unknown father. Was that also an arranged coupling?

Why did Sieglinde feel the need to bring her long-held secret into the open now?

Thomas shook his head. "Well, I guess I will try to find out more. There was a program, *Lebensborn*, that no one knew about, a secret that was kept by the women who participated. They wanted to do their part for the Third Reich by giving Hitler babies to populate his vision."

Thomas veered towards his mother's home where he was spending the night.

As Michael and I walked to our hotel, we kept glancing at each other. Finally, Michael stopped, held out his hands. He pointed to mine, so I held them out. Both sets short and stubby.

"See, we are definitely related," Michael grinned. And we stood in the street, guffawing our discomfort away.

What difference does this knowledge make in our relationships to each other? Sieglinde was still my ebullient aunt; her three boys full of life and warmth. Michael was still my beloved cousin with a huge heart, the one who could make me double over in laughter about pretty much anything. Aunt Christel's face still split easily into a grin, even as her eyes rolled at something she found silly. None of whom and what they were had changed. And my uncle, well, he was born after Felix died, so we always knew he had a different father, although his mother never revealed who. But I had always assumed that Opa Felix was the father of the five girls, and the grandfather of their children.

As our trip continued, Sieglinde's confession drifted away like a will-o-the-wisp. I was unsure if I wanted to pull this revelation into the sunlight and give it substance. Better to let it cower in the shadows. After all, it wasn't as if anything could be changed. As a teen, I had grappled with my German heritage. Books and movies about the Nazi regime had struck me deeply. Childhood memories, of a loving Oma, and the simple life we lived together, did not reconcile with the horrors I eventually learned about. I knew my family had lived through them, but I refused to make the connection. I wanted to believe they had been far removed from the hatred, fear, and pogroms that took place.

Yet, a little voice nagged at me, deep in the recesses of a mind that needed to understand. That voice kept whispering for the next three years. Family and business back home demanded attention; kept me busy enough to shush the voice into an obscure corner. I spoke to my cousins sporadically. Occasionally the subject of Sieglinde's revelation came up.

Finally, the voice became a mantra. I called Cousin Thomas and told him I wanted to learn more, to understand what had happened in our family. I wanted to write our story and create a legacy of truth. Could he please ask his mother if she would share her story with us? After all, she had opened up at the café for reasons we didn't understand yet. Perhaps the time was ripe now to pull us into this part of our family history. The history that no one had questioned out loud.

Some family secrets are meant to be kept silent. I wondered once again if we could—should—leave this one alone, this secret that had remained buried for seventy-seven years. The voice insisted it was time.

Sieglinde agreed.

•

Early June 2016

As I packed suitcases for a trip to Germany three years after Sieglinde shared her secret, I wondered, once again, about my own father. I had no memory of him, only the knowledge that my mother never married him, and took me out of his life at birth. Even as a child I intuited that he was a forbidden subject. The questions I asked my mother were met with anger and guilt.

I knew where he lived because I had tried to contact him, once.

In the spring of 2009, shortly before my fifty-fourth birthday, my stepfather Ted died from bladder cancer. Grief-stricken, Mom sent his son, my half-brother Patrick, a packet of his papers to go through, mostly military records and awards from an illustrious career. Tucked into the stack, probably inadvertently, were old, mimeographed papers in German. Patrick sent these to me. When the paperwork arrived, I saw they were official court documents dealing with my birth. Within the faded pages, I read that my biological German father acknowledged his paternity, agreed to pay monthly support to my mother until I turned sixteen, and relinquished all rights to me.

Now I very much wanted—no, needed—to find this father. I called Michael and asked if he could track him down with the name and old address that I now had. He called all the listed names in the surrounding area, with no luck. Finally, he wrote to the city hall of my father's town listed on the paperwork. A few weeks later, they wrote back and provided a forwarding address. Michael found a phone number and made a call.

Then Michael called me. He stumbled over his words, trying to find kind ones.

"He doesn't understand why now, after all this time, you're contacting him. He says he doesn't want to go back and remember that painful period in his life. He's sorry, but it's too late."

I had taken the call in my husband's office, surrounded by piles of paperwork, CDs, and work files all stacked high. Walls and shelves were crammed full of framed family pictures: in our boat when our sixteen-year-old son was still a toddler; of Jay and his soccer coach; the three of us pointing fake radar guns at the monsters on the Men in Black ride at Universal Studios. A handmade Best Dad award was proudly displayed on the wall.

I swiveled back and forth in the oversized office chair and swallowed the bile of rejection that had crept into my throat.

"It's ok, Michael. I haven't really lost anything. You can't lose what you don't have."

•

More silence. More secrets. I never approached Mom with the discovery of my father's identity. She suffered from ailments related to anxiety and COPD and I saw no point in bringing up this part of our past; she had never wanted to talk about it. My father had rejected me, so perhaps my mother had good reason to be silent about him. I also lost the chance to talk to her about her sister's revelation.

After my stepfather died, we moved Mom to Colorado to live in my half-sister Jackie's large built-out basement suite. I had plans to fly to Colorado that July to mom-sit while Jackie and her family went on vacation. I hoped to talk to her about Sieglinde's confession. Mom was six when her sister was born. What had she seen, or heard? I also hoped to ask her, once again, about my father. But fate intervened. She died of pneumonia a few weeks before my scheduled trip.

What happens when we find out much—most—of what we always believed about our family is not so; when we are handed multiple options as truth? How do we decide which one to choose? Which one fits best into the life story we carry for ourselves and those we love?

"We tell ourselves stories in order to live … We interpret what we see; select the most workable of the multiple choices," offers the writer Joan Didion.

What stories do wartime, poverty, hunger, and a broken family create? What would my grandmother tell me if we could sit down and talk openly about the choices she made? What about my mother? What could she have told me, honestly, about her choices, about leaving her child behind? And what about my unknown father? Was he still alive, and healthy? Could I try again to meet him, and by doing so find closure for the yearning I've always felt? Questions I had worked hard at avoiding piled up.

So began a journey of discovery.

We had stumbled upon a bond, Sieglinde and I: two fatherless children growing up at different times, affected by decisions made by other people, which shaped our lives and determined our identities. We needed to understand our mothers, and the choices they made. We needed to know who our fathers were so that we may finally know who we are. Yes, it's another story that will fan the flames in Hitler's hell. But it is, first and foremost, a story of family affected by *those times*, and the choices that were made. It is also a story of self-discovery.

When I asked Sieglinde why now, why bring up the painful specter of this part of her otherwise fulfilling life, she banged her fist on the table, and with eyes sparking stated, "Ich will die Wahrheit!" I want the truth to be known.

My aunt's confession became the catalyst that sent me traveling back and forth between my childhood country and my home in Florida for four years, beginning in 2016. During this time, I met new relatives and visited places connected to my childhood which prompted old memories to rise. It seemed everyone had a story for me that brought history to life. As I discovered my maternal family, a parallel path took me back into my own history, and the father I thought I had never known.

At night, dreams were filled with images seen through a child's eyes: my beloved Oma, who held me in her arms as my mother carried her suitcases down the stairs and out of my life. Images of Oma's and my plain but cozy home. Of our large garden and of the surrounding countryside in a small farm town. My short history as a German child before everything changed.

When I had [illegible] during the [illegible] of [illegible] [illegible] [illegible] Little and [illegible] [illegible] the truth to be known.

My adult [illegible] confessed [illegible] that sent me [illegible] back [illegible] between my childhood country and my [illegible] in [illegible] for four years beginning in [illegible]. During this time, I [illegible] my relatives and visited places connected to my childhood, which prompted old memories [illegible]. [illegible] everyone had a story [illegible] [illegible] history [illegible]. As I [illegible] my material, a [illegible] parallel [illegible] took me back into my own history and the father I thought I had left forever.

[illegible] dreams were filled with images seen through a child's eyes, my beloved Cuba, who [illegible] [illegible] my [illegible] [illegible] [illegible] images of Cuba and my [illegible] home [illegible] and of the surrounding countryside in a small [illegible] town [illegible] history [illegible] could [illegible] everything changed.

PART 1
FOUNDATION

"Destiny is a name often given in retrospect to choices that had dramatic consequences."
J.K. Rowling

The Yearning

The child's left foot pushes the paved road. She's riding her scooter where she's not supposed to: on the main road through a neighborhood far from home. An inner voice tells her to turn around and race downhill for familiar streets. She doesn't listen. There is adventure here, so she keeps going, up to a place she's not been before. She is five years old.

Here are the nice houses. Unlike Oma's hulking stucco quadplex, shared with three other families, only one family lives in each home here. Prim hedges line the lawns. Gardens drip with roses and hydrangeas. There are no neat utilitarian rows of vegetables here.

High-pitched whimpering stops her. Following the direction of the cries, the little girl spots a glorious sight on the front porch of a large home: a basket filled with a white fluffy dog surrounded by her puppies, each jostling for a spot on their mother's belly. Sunshine warms the cool air. She stands at the end of the walkway, her body vibrating, delirious with want. Not because she wants a puppy; she wants to *be* one of those puppies, cuddling in the warmth. She is not allowed to go up to this house. She doesn't know anyone here.

After glancing around, her treacherous feet dance towards the basket. Her right hand reaches out to stroke a tiny warm round belly. The puppies' eyes are still closed, bodies pink and quivering. One, two, three, four, and five! Before her mind can register the growl, sharp intense pain blurs her eyesight. When it clears, she finds herself back down the walkway, fingers dripping bright red blood. Screaming, she runs to her scooter, flips it around and pushes off for home.

Her rattled brain yells at her as she flies downhill: *you weren't supposed to be there, you were supposed to only ride back and forth on Kantstrasse, in front of your home; you weren't supposed to go up to a strange house; you weren't supposed to touch a strange dog that bites you; you will get yelled at and sent to lie down. Oma will get that sad, tired look in her eyes again.*

Oma gasps and asks what happened. The child mumbles that she fell off her scooter. The brand-new red scooter with shiny silver wheels that was a gift from the woman she was told is her mother. The woman who visited at Christmas but left again. The child says she's sorry and squints hopefully into her grandmother's face. Oma stares closely at the bitten fingers. Stares hard into those lying eyes. Sighs. That sad, tired look returns. The girl gets that hollow feeling in her stomach again, the one that makes her feel bad about herself. Oma washes off the blood, wraps fingers in bandages and sends the girl to lie down, after all.

•

A yearning for a mother's touch, that belly of warmth and security, had me reach out and touch those puppies. This antic of mine matches up with what Mom told me, much later, about being a restless, anxious child, prone to mishaps. What I do remember is living with a chronic low-thrumming anxiety, a sense of something not being right. Did I overhear talk, perhaps between Oma and the neighbor who sometimes came for coffee: a low murmur about the difficulties of raising a *bänkling kind,* an accidental child who acted as if she were her own dominion? One who, literally, thumbed her nose at authority? It's likely I did.

Grandmothers aren't supposed to be mothers; they are the ones who spoil a child, not raise her. But there I was, with no parents to speak of. My single mother traveled the world performing in clubs as a dancer. My biological father was denied access at my mother's request. I didn't know these things at the time.

I may have yearned for a mother, but what I strongly remember is wanting a father, *my* father. It was an overwhelming feeling as strong as hunger and thirst combined. A need that could not be sated. When it hit, I would pull the kitchen stool to the front window, straddle it and stare with unwavering intensity at our front walk, willing a man to walk down it, ring the doorbell and claim me. It would be a tall stranger who would tell me how he had been searching for me. That he loved me and wanted me. A father.

I would sit until the feeling passed. Sometimes it seemed like hours. Other times I would run down two flights of stairs and wedge myself between the root vegetable bins in our dark, dank cellar to listen to the silence, until the noise of it became unbearable. Then it was time to go outside, to the garden. I would sit between the rows of ripening strawberry plants, head lifted to soak up the sun, or play hide and seek with my invisible friend Mebbie, amongst the raspberry vines, or climb over the thorny gooseberry bushes trying not to get pricked. Or wander the meadow downhill by the river, jumping up to snatch crab-apples off low branches; eating until the ache in my stomach replaced the hollowness in my chest.

Snails were lovingly collected and placed in a shoebox filled with sticks and grass and flowers. They were named: Bummi, Putzi, or Max and Moritz, after the children's books Oma read to me. Once, just once, I collected ferocious looking black beetles and brought them home, pockets buzzing loudly until I released the insects in our kitchen. A screaming Oma shooed them out of an open window.

Our flat was upstairs, the kitchen long and narrow with a black iron wood-burning stove. Our bedroom was just off the kitchen. I slept with Oma in a bed covered with snow-white sheets and a goose-down comforter, dreaming those dreams only children dream. My clothes were nestled next to Oma's in a massive walnut armoire on the wall opposite our bed. In the warmer months, Oma kept the casement windows that covered most of one bedroom wall open to the fresh air. On sunny mornings she hung our comforter on the window ledge.

I had a real friend named Jutta who lived directly across the way, in an upstairs quadplex identical to ours. On long summer evenings, after we had been put to bed, we would hang out of our windows and holler across at each other, then fall into fits of laughter like only two little girls could, our giggles rolling out of us, making us cough and sputter and lose our breath. It never took long for Oma to come flying in, shaking her head and threatening to call for the bedtime owl to pay a visit. The owl was a favorite bogeyman, one that sat and stared at children who refused to go to sleep. I held a fearful fascination of owls for years.

From the front entrance of the quadplex, a mahogany staircase led to our apartment door. This opened into a small foyer. A formal parlor was to the left of it, used for visitors and afternoon *kaffe-trinken.* To the right was our bathroom, which contained a claw-footed tub and a toilet with a chain I could barely reach to flush water from the overhead tank.

•

The shimmering afternoon sun shines through a large window. Fingers of warmth reach into a long narrow room that serves as kitchen and family room. The child, perhaps three or four years old, lies on an aged cloth divan tucked up against the wall behind a worn Formica table. Her grandmother is not here in this room, nor is she in the bedroom. She could be in the parlor or even the attic. She could be in the garden collecting vegetables to make soup for the evening meal.

The restless girl is expected to take a nap. Or at least to lie quietly. She hums something tuneless, makes noises with her lips. She's bored. Watches the sunlight as it taps on the ceiling, an edge of the table, top of the buffet. A mild breeze through a slightly open window brings in whiffs of warm dirt and grass. It must be late spring or summer. The child wants to be outside, but she has been outside all morning; her sagging knee socks are striated with brown dirt. She places her feet flat on the divan, props one leg on top of a knee, and begins to bounce her foot.

A glint on the buffet catches her attention. The sun is highlighting something new, something interesting. Something to make time go by faster. She sits up and listens. All's quiet as she slips down and crab-crawls under the table to the kitchen door. Puts her ear to it. Hazards a quick glance through a glass panel which makes up the top part of the door. The foyer is empty. She tiptoes to the buffet and gasps. Look! There is a small pile of coins, rare in this poor house. Mostly they are copper, probably *pfennigs*. She picks them up. They fill her tiny hand.

The girl slides back under the table, back onto the divan. The coins clink marvelously when she rolls them in her fingers. She places her feet back on the divan and props her foot back onto her knee. Bounce, hum, clink. She thinks about how important this money is. How Oma always worries about never having enough. She holds her moneyed fist over her face and starts to drop the coins one by one to catch them with her mouth. Mostly she misses, but two go in.

At this moment the kitchen door opens with a screech and Oma's heavy breathing enters the room. She is winded from the two flights of stairs she has just climbed. The girl's heart lurches, and she swallows as she sits up too quickly. There may be a moment of silence before the screaming begins. As her Oma rushes to her, the frightened girl holds out her closed fist, leftover coins poking through her fingers. She whacks her stomach with the fist of coins while screaming. Oma knows something has happened, but it takes a few minutes before cries turn to hiccups and finally, to an explanation. And a question.

"Oma, will I die now?"

Oma looks relieved, angry, sad, resigned. She shakes her pale blonde head slowly and assures her grandchild that no, she probably will not die. For the next two days, the girl must carry a wooden spoon with her when she goes to the bathroom. The coins are washed and reused. The girl lives. Her Oma sighs that same tired sigh.

•

Our three-room flat came with additional attic space of two rooms with loft ceilings lit by dingy slat windows. To get there, I had to climb the polished mahogany stairs, aided by a curving banister. One room contained the dusty, mysterious accumulations of the last twenty years. Here were boxes filled with game boards and pieces, dolls with sparse hair and missing limbs, old clothes, perhaps a dark wooden stool with only two legs. In the second room, beds had at one time been lined up in a row for Oma's children. The room did not seem large enough to hold the dreams of so many. Dreams in *those times*, the time of war and uncertainty, were luxuries snatched in odd moments and held fast for fear they would dissipate. I didn't know this then, yet I must have felt the whispers of those yearnings.

Or perhaps they were all mine. Imagination ran wild as I thought about the children who once slept here. I found the attic creepy and wondered if they had, too. I now imagine Aunt Sieglinde as a child, wandering the rooms as I did. Feeling the anxiety as I did. Something was not right, something essential was missing from this home. It was a home without a father. Until a boy was born many years later, this was a home filled with dresses and pinafores, white socks and Mary Jane shoes, barrettes, and ribbons to fasten tight braids.

Little Sieglinde's questions about a father went unanswered while her mother struggled to support the family. She cleaned government offices and mended clothes for the officers in town. How many of them knew the long-legged, golden-haired Katharina whose children slept in the attic? I imagine late night callers in uniform leaving behind a whiff of tobacco, or perhaps a scent of pomade on the pillow in the bed with the white down comforter.

I knew Katharina as Oma. The person who cared for me. She exuded a weariness that made her seem older than a woman in her mid-forties. Yet Oma offered me a quiet home, her guidance a constant foil to those reckless ways I tended towards. I never felt much like I belonged to anyone, but I knew that safety and love came from her. It's likely I overheard talk about a mother I had somewhere, or perhaps Oma had sat me down at some point and explained what must have been incomprehensible to my child's mind: that I have a mother but she cannot live with me, she cannot care for me.

I lived life outdoors, doing things that got me dirty. Things that boys did. My shins stayed bruised from climbing trees, fingernails grubby from the garden. I wished I was a boy. Boys seemed to have a freedom that girls didn't. They also became fathers when they grew up. Fathers were a mystery to me because I didn't know any. My best friend Jutta only had a mother, sister and brother; my aunts had husbands or boyfriends but no children yet. I stared at families when Oma and I did our shopping in town. Seeing families with fathers made me dizzy with interest. And yearning.

Hans Herbert, the youngest of Oma's six children, was nine when I came to live with her at the age of five months. Once I could, I toddled along behind him, this grinning, swaggering boy who picked on me mercilessly. I was five when he started culinary school. He quickly became an apprentice and moved away. He came home periodically, a lanky teenager with an Elvis pompadour and a carefully parted duck's ass, his plump lips curled in an insolent grin. I would stick my face in his and declare, "I'm gonna marry you when I grow up, Onkel Hans," give him a determined look, and collapse into giggles.

Occasionally one of the aunts would come by, usually with gifts. It's possible that Aunt Christel brought me the roller skates I rode up and down our sidewalk. Old photos show me with both Sieglinde and Christel, a hula hoop around a skinny waist. But mostly Oma and I lived in our little bubble. She was patient with me. I don't recall getting spanked or disciplined with demeaning words. If she regretted being stuck with me, she never showed it.

Oma taught me to crochet a scarf. To mend a sock with a red wooden darning egg that I somehow, miraculously, have today. She showed me how to give myself a manicure, sharing with me her small case that contained nail scissors, a cuticle pusher and a metal nail file. I would sit on her lap and dig the dirt from the garden out from under my nails, then file the ragged edges until they were smooth. At night, before bedtime, we both dipped our fingers into the blue canister of Nivea cream and rubbed it into our elbows, heels, and hands. In the mornings, we would stroll together between the rows of vegetables in our garden. I plucked or pulled out of the ground what we needed for our afternoon meal. I helped scrub the carrots and potatoes with a brush, carefully picked any bugs out of the lettuce, washed the leaves, and put aside the tender yellow hearts for my own salad.

One snowy December day in 1960, when I was five years old, a vision appeared at our front door. I stared up at her and thought of a doll: a porcelain face with blue eyes and bud lips, and a cloud of dark hair illuminated by the light from the open doorway greeted me. The woman beamed at me. One of her front teeth was chipped in a crooked line. Her arms were filled with brightly wrapped gifts. A faint, smoky smell of cigarettes swirled around her. Oma introduced her as "deine Mutti." Your mother. Behind her stood a wide man in a dark green uniform, legs splayed, arms crossed in front of his ample girth as he squinted down at me. His teeth clenched a pipe, his brown eyes were warm and inquisitive.

In the formal parlor, I was placed in the man's lap. "Das ist dein neuer Papa," my mother explained. I wiggled nervously, fascinated by this new daddy's uniform, and babbled away with questions about the pins and ribbons on his jacket. He remained silent, frowning slightly. I trembled with excitement, looked back and forth between these parents I had so extraordinarily been gifted with. Yet my chest began to feel thick, and my gut twisted in fear. In a moment, I understood. I twisted around to stare at Oma. I knew life was about to change.

Madeleine, 1958

A New Life

On June 29th 1961, my mother Susi got married in a small military ceremony in Frankfurt. I was six years old and stayed with my maternal great-grandparents at their home in Bavaria while Oma and two of Mom's sisters and their husbands attended the wedding. The only photo I've seen was taken after the ceremony: Susi is smiling into the camera, her chipped front tooth adding charm to her carefully made-up face. The smile does not reach her eyes; they appear tired and uncertain. A delicate veil drapes over her shoulders to her waist, and she holds a bouquet of blood red carnations. The neckline on her simple white dress is high; a white lace petticoat peeks out from the hemline that barely touches her knees. Her new husband supports her right hand. His large brown eyes are warm and proud: presenting Chief Warrant Officer and Mrs. Ted L. McKrill.

After their honeymoon, the three of us moved to the Army Post in Frankfurt where I began first grade. I knew a few words of English, mainly please, thank you, and horse. Most memories of the first two years of school are buried somewhere in my subconscious. Occasionally, an image will pop up. Studies have shown that stress can interfere with long-term memory formation; my low-grade chronic stress certainly reached a peak in those years. As I learned the English language, notes from teachers pleaded that I learn to communicate with my new words instead of my fists. I guess it was easier, and quicker, to quieten the taunts of classmates physically instead of stumbling through words I didn't know well. Instead of trying to make friends, I tilted a defiant chin at those who stared and whispered amongst themselves, or glanced my way, snickering.

Tall, thin, with bowl-cut hair, I still wore German dresses and sturdy shoes. My right eye was crossed, and I wore cat-eyeglasses. One day I came home and asked Mom what it meant to "cross-side". She looked at me in confusion and said it meant to move over. I squinted back at her in frustration and said that couldn't be, because other kids referred to me as *being* cross-side. That evening as I lay in bed, I heard strained voices drifting from the kitchen. A few days later we visited an ophthalmologist. Soon after, I had surgery to tighten the eye muscles and align the pupil. But it was too late to correct my vision. I've never had good spatial ability or depth perception.

One memory stands out clearly, probably from first grade because I have a strong sense of not speaking English yet. I'm running, delirious with adrenalin. The taste of winning forces a bark of laughter as I turn my head to look over a shoulder at a classmate when WHOP! Darkness.

Pain brings me around with a gasp. I look up into a sea of blurry faces as my head splits into a thousand pieces. They tell me I came to several times, vomited, and went back under, mercifully for me but frightening for the teachers who rushed me to the Army hospital. When I swim back to consciousness, my mother and new stepfather are hovering over me. The look on their faces frightens me more than the pain. The PAIN. A mask and the cloying smell of chloroform takes it, and me, away again. When I wake up, it's in a white room, on white sheets, white cotton gauze wrapped around my head and part of my face mummy-style. My six-year-old brain struggles to remember.

The first-grade classes of Frankfurt American School #1 had caravanned by bus to a local park for fresh air and sports. Taller than most of my classmates, I loved running, long legs able to gobble up the ground. As I struggled to fit in, I jumped at every chance to prove my worth at something—anything to detract from the lack of words and American ways I had yet to learn. A race was called and a group of us lined up. The race began. A rock seemed to come out of nowhere and gashed the top of my head open over the left eye. I ended up with a concussion and required a multitude of stitches.

They told us it had been an errant rock thrown by someone for their dog to fetch. I try hard to think. I cannot recall anyone outside of our class being around. Certainly not a dog. I would remember a dog. What stands out in strobe-like images from that event is the look on my mother's face: of doubt, fear, and anger.

•

My stepfather Ted and I eased around each other carefully. Mostly I tried to avoid him, this over-sized man who didn't speak my language. I would catch his thoughtful eyes on me, then look away, as uncomfortable as I was. He did win a piece of my heart by teaching me to ride a bicycle. I still had that red scooter with the shiny wheels, but what I wanted more than anything was a bike. Day and night, I badgered these new parents, as I flounced around and sighed dramatically with desire. Mom told me I needed to wait another year or so, until I was seven. It was Ted who came home early one day with a shiny new bike strapped to the back of his Buick. We took it to the grassy area behind our apartment and I climbed on. The smiles were huge on both our faces the first time I held my balance.

Mostly though, he went to work, came home for supper, and watched our little black and white television. Not one prone to chit-chat, his large brown eyes underneath bushy brows observed everything and everyone, his bulk solid and unmoving. He was not the dad that swung you onto his shoulders and told you silly stories. He adored Mom and demanded respect, quick to pull off his belt and flail my butt whenever he caught me sassing her.

For years, the questions I asked about my biological father went unanswered as Mom skittered away from me, smell of acrid cigarette smoke following. Why couldn't she have been happy with my German father and raise me in the country we both knew so well? Who was he exactly? What did he do? One summer day, shortly after my fifteenth birthday, I stood in front of her, hands on hips, legs splayed to keep from trembling. "Mom, it's time you told me about my real father, who he was and what he was like. And why you guys didn't get married."

She squinted up at me as she knelt in the garden pulling weeds, an ashy Lucky Strike dangling from the side of her mouth.

"Why are you asking? Daddy is your real father. It would hurt his feelings if he thought you didn't think of him that way," she muttered in her still-heavy German accent and turned her attention back to the yard.

I walked away, telling myself it didn't matter, anyway. I hated being German, I hated my mother's sharp looks and her even sharper tongue, her clipped words with *th* sounding like *d*, and *v* sounding like *f*. Why did I even care about my German father, who was not involved in my life? She did toss out a few facts: he wore glasses (*he had bad eyes—that's where you got your eye problems from)*, he worked as a typesetter *(you probably got your love of books from him)*, he wasn't very good-looking (here she just looked closely at my face) and *he had not much to offer; not much at all. He asked me to marry him, but I said no. I would have been nothing more than a putzfrau, cooking and cleaning.*

My teenage mind reeled with confusion at these biting words. Choosing to ignore what I could not understand or change, I buried my father deep in a mental file, and with him a part of myself that was unknowable. By this time I had also let go of my German history, along with the woman who had taken me in when my mother left me behind, my Oma, Katharina.

A Wedding Portrait

In an old photo album is the only photograph of my grandparents. It is their wedding day. My grandfather Felix stands erect and solemn, pale blue eyes soft and deep-set in his angular face, the aquiline nose prominent above thin lips that hint at a smile. He is in his *Heeren* uniform, chest pocket bedecked with pins. His left hand clutches a pair of white gloves and his peaked *Shirmutze,* the crossed swords prominent under an eagle insignia. His right arm appears to be in the small of his bride's back. Katharina is leaning ever so slightly towards him, her left foot firm and sure, her right heel off the ground as she tilts, toe out for support.

My grandmother is lovely: blonde hair in tight curls frame her face, which is make-up free except for a touch of light lipstick; pale lashes make her blue eyes large and luminous. A girl in love on her wedding day. She wears a simple white satin dress that allows matching pumps to peek out. A long gossamer veil, bordered by a vine of tiny roses, flows from a beaded tiara and cascades onto the floor in a semi-circle beside her. A delicate teardrop chain drapes her neck. She is holding in her white-gloved hands a bouquet of white roses and lacy greenery.

The photo haunts me because I know their tragic history. What are they thinking? What are they feeling? What hopes do they have for the future? Are they madly in love? I think so. Look at how Katharina leans towards him, into him. Giving herself.

•

Katharina Renner and Felix Fornoff on their wedding day in 1933.

My Oma Katharina met her future husband Felix in Amberg, a small city about twelve kilometers southeast of Rosenberg in Bavaria. They may have met at a dance, in the year 1930 or '31. Rosenberg had not much to offer besides billowing smoke and noise from the steel mill where her father worked. Katharina would have headed to Amberg for a bit of social life, or perhaps to flirt with the soldiers who were stationed there. She probably walked the seven or so miles to get there, since her family had no transportation, and the train ticket would have been costly. I envision her purposeful march in sensible lace-up shoes, a precious pair of kitten heels tucked in her bag for later, a scarf tied over her carefully coiffed hair to keep the dust off. Perhaps a farmer with his horse and wagon came by and offered her a ride. Perhaps she rode a bicycle on warm summer nights. However she made her way, she and Felix found one another, most likely at a dance.

I imagine a large club. The doors are open to the early dusk as a local band plays traditional *Volksmusik*. Lights are haloed softly within the smoky interior. Felix stands rigid and handsome in his army uniform, cigarette smoke curling up from his left hand. Katharina is lovely, perhaps a bit mysterious. A meticulous seamstress, she knew how to accentuate her long lines in stylish home-made dresses. There she stands, gazing appraisingly around the dance hall, her sensible walking shoes now replaced with the kitten heels, the scarf with a jaunty hat. She taps a foot to the music. In the northern cities such as Berlin and Hamburg, American jazz had made an impact. But in Bavaria, dancing the *Schuhplattler*, a dance of rigorous knee and heel smacking while dressed in *lederhosen* and knee socks, would have been the dance of the day for the men. Polka music would have been on the agenda, allowing couples to hold hands and gaze into each other's eyes as they twirled around the dance floor.

Perhaps he saw her first, across that hazy room, the soft lights casting halos into her golden hair. Or it could be she had her eyes on him first, drawn by his firm stance and steely gaze. A man of strength. One she can lean into. She allows her look to linger just a moment too long before she coquettishly looks down. She pulls a cigarette out of her purse, slowly, to give him time to cross the space between them. He offers a light and comments on the music. She smiles and nods, starts to tap her foot again. He bows slightly and offers his arm as they head onto the dance floor.

Sadly, the rest of their love story is lost. What we do know is that Felix and Katharina came together. But Felix was not welcome at the Renner's home; Katharina's father Martin did not like him. What is not known is the exact reason. It's possible that Martin did not want his daughter dating a career soldier. He may have had bigger plans for his beloved firstborn. It may have been that an offer of marriage did not come quickly enough when Katharina found herself pregnant with my mother Susi, and gave birth in 1932.

Katharina was a woman in love. But it wasn't until she became pregnant again that an offer of marriage came from Felix. They moved into military housing in Deggendorf, a town a few hours away. My mother was almost two when the second daughter Gunda was born in 1934. Erika followed in 1936. Felix was often deployed to oversee the building of military housing in other parts of the country as Hitler grew his armed forces. Katharina and her girls stayed behind in Deggendorf.

I think about Katharina's life as she settled into raising her family, away from the only home she had ever known. An absent husband who came home often enough to leave her pregnant as he went off on another tour. Did she find support in her neighbors, in other military wives who shared her loneliness? Was she satisfied with her life, or did she want more? In an old photo album, there are several photos of her taken with her girls. Katharina wears fashionable dresses with clean lines, or a wool coat and a jaunty hat on her tightly coiffed hair. The girls, Susi, Erika, and Gunda, are in frilly dresses and pinafores, their hair freshly combed and held back by barrettes. It appears she is presenting her family, showing her accomplishments as a wife and mother.

My old photo album also has several pages filled with pictures of Katharina at their military home in Deggendorf during this time. Her three girls play on the front steps with toy figures, balls and dolls. She is smiling down on them fondly. I know now what her loose dress and long apron are covering up: Katharina is pregnant with her fourth child, Sieglinde. Soon after this photo was taken, she packed up and readied herself and the girls to move to the new home her husband Felix built in the small farmer town of Montabaur. He does not know Katharina is pregnant again. He has not been home in many months.

Susi, Katharina, Erika, and Gunda. Deggendorf circa 1938

PART 2
DISCOVERY

"To be rooted is perhaps the most important and least recognized need of the human soul."
Simone Weil

Finding Papa

Bad Nauheim
June 2016

Cousin Michael and I shift from foot to foot as we gape up at the tall apartment building. At black and once-white bricks in need of washing. At a door that's locked. At the name tag underneath the doorbell, handwritten in blue ink, slanted and faded. We're here after dropping my twenty-four-year-old son Jay at the Frankfurt Airport after our jaunt over to Iceland. We've been traveling together. He's flying home to Florida today but I'm staying for another month. In little more than a week, Michael and I will drive to Thomas' house in Munich where Aunt Sieglinde will tell us the rest of her story. Of finding her father.

Michael, his wife Ivonne and I have been discussing my own father, and how he turned down the chance to meet me when Michael contacted him back in 2009. I had thought about contacting him again, but the hopeless rejection I felt when I received the fateful call from Michael telling me that my father had refused a meeting deterred me. I wasn't sure I could take a face-to-face dismissal.

As we left the airport, Michael turned inquisitive blue eyes on me.

"What do think about just ringing your father's doorbell? I have his address. It's not far from here. You never know; he may have changed his mind by now and be happy to see you. Of course, he may also not be alive anymore."

Heart thumping, I agreed. I wasn't sure what would be worse: that he had died, and I would never even know what he looked like, or if he would turn me away. Yet I thought to myself, why not? I have nothing to lose at this point. Michael put his address into the navigation system and here we were.

Both of us are wide-eyed and dry-mouthed. Hesitating.

Now what, I implore Michael, with a raised eyebrow. Footsteps echo inside. The door opens as a bespectacled middle-aged man comes out, whistling, car keys in hand. I grab the door before it closes behind him, some part of my paralyzed brain thinking I may get brave enough to dash upstairs.

"Kann ich Ihnen helfen?" he asks politely. May I help you?

Michael quickly explains who we are here to see; our families are old friends. Does he still live here? Is he well?

"Yes, he's doing well and lives with his wife on the third floor."

Without preamble, the helpful neighbor reaches past me to push the button.

Oh, no. I'm not ready for this.

Six, seven, eight rings; I need to suck in air, but can't. *No one's home*!

A guttural voice comes through the intercom, "Ja?" The neighbor explains that old friends are downstairs. The voice says he's coming right down.

A roar in my head renders me mute as I look helplessly at Michael, whose eyes are darting around like he's thinking about dashing away. The clueless neighbor stands by, smiling and happy to be of assistance.

Footsteps clop down the stairs. I'm still holding the entrance door as an elderly man appears in front of us. His welcome smile fades as he swivels on the balls of his feet, and peers at Michael and me in turn, clearly puzzled. We all stand there, awkward and silent. The neighbor's smile begins to fade, his eyes on me, questioning. I need him to leave. I don't want any witnesses. He finally heads to his car, glances back over his left shoulder, brow furrowed now with curiosity or concern.

My father and I are both in the doorway as he turns to me. Eyes the color of bleached denim search mine. We are almost the same height. I stand tall, lift my head, and say the words in German I have been practicing over and over on the way: "Ich bin deine Tochter." I am your daughter. My father sways just a bit, and I see in his eyes that the millisecond before I said this, he already knew.

•

My father turns shakily and motions us in and up to his flat. The three of us crowd into a tiny lift. We are in such proximity that I don't know where to look. Every nerve ending is lit up. The air is sparking. We reach the third floor and pile out. Father fumbles to put the key in the keyhole. We enter a narrow hallway and Michael and I follow him to the room at the end.

The living room of the modest apartment is suffused with light from a wall of large windows. A brown parquet floor is crisscrossed with muted oriental rugs. Shelves groan with books and framed photos. Succulents and orchids thrive on a spacious windowsill amidst groupings of knick-knacks that look like they have been gathered from around the world: a hand-carved giraffe, a colorful African basket, a small blue Buddha.

My father falls into a well-worn beige recliner. He will turn ninety this year but appears much younger. Eyes crinkle and disappear when he smiles. Like mine, I realize with a jolt. Michael and I back slowly onto the front edge of a small divan and gingerly sit down. I'm looking at a man I've tried to envision a thousand times.

He lifts himself heavily out of the recliner and goes to a cabinet, digs through a box. Finds an envelope and pulls out a letter, which he places in front of me. He hands Michael the envelope and points to the address.

"Michael, after your phone call those years ago, I thought about the conversation. I was shocked with myself that my first reaction was to say no, I don't want to meet my daughter now; it has been too long. I didn't have a phone number for you, so I looked online for information and found an address."

Father points to the envelope, now creased and worn.

"Here, this is where I sent the letter. Is this an old address? It took a few weeks for it to come back undeliverable. You can see that I asked if you could please have my daughter contact me. And I put in my regret at turning her away at first."

Michael tells him this is an old address, from many years ago. Father shakes his head and looks at me, eyes moist and warm. My own eyes well up and relief floods through me. Followed by regret. Seven years ago! I could have rung his bell seven years ago. If only I had been brave enough to get his address and phone number from Michael and pursued a meeting. But all I had felt was rejection. I had let the chance go.

Our impetuous visit today suddenly feels like destiny.

Father asks how my mother is. I explain that she died three years ago, at eighty, after battling COPD and emphysema. He lowers his eyes, as if offering up a moment of silence. Then he begins his story. One I've waited a lifetime to hear.

•

On a bright summer day in 1953, Susanna Fornoff walked into the print shop where my father had worked as a typesetter ever since his 1947 release as a prisoner of war. She was looking for part-time work, to supplement her modeling assignments and waitressing work. She was hired. My father was smitten.

"Susi was very pretty, with dark hair, a bright smile and those high heels! I was shocked when she agreed to go out with me. Ha! I was more shocked that I had nerve enough to ask her—I was a simple man with nothing to offer. *Ach*, we were young and wild, zipping around on my motorcycle. She was only twenty-three, six years younger than me."

He stares into the near distance, seeing images I can't begin to imagine.

Until he digs in a cabinet and pulls out a worn photo album, which he places gently in my lap. Monochrome pictures of a woman I don't recognize until suddenly I do: a smiling young woman with a cloud of wavy dark hair framing a face flush with vitality. Her eyes gaze flirtatiously into the lens. She is glowing. In a striped tube top, knee high riding boots and large pearl earrings, sitting cross-legged on a motorcycle. Leaning gracefully on a ship's railing, in an A-line dress with oversized front pockets, tiny waist accented by a thin leather belt. With Father, both in bathing suits, lolling beside a lake. Page after page.

My young Papa looks like the proverbial cat who has just swallowed a mouse. Mom looks happier than I had ever seen her. Than I ever thought she could be. The woman in the photos has the world by the tail and swings it fearlessly while yelling yee-haw at the top of her lungs. She is strong and confident. Her eyes sparkle with life, at once challenging and engaging the camera and the man behind it.

I'm stunned. This is a woman I never knew.

Early memories must have noted this vibrant woman. She was the one who showed up that fateful December day at Oma's door, excited to become an American officer's wife. As the image of her large smile drifts back into my mind's eye, I realize how quickly and completely I had forgotten that woman. The father I had never known has now brought her back to me. Suddenly I'm a child again, with the empty feeling of desiring something I don't understand, crouching in the cellar or sitting for hours staring at the front walk. A wave of new understanding hits me: the longing for a father was simpler than the longing for a mother. I knew everyone had a mother, and, as I noted other families, I accepted that not everyone had fathers. But the rejection of a mother was unacceptable. When my mother returned to claim me from Oma, some part of me did not trust her.

My father continues his story. He is not in this room with us anymore; he is deep in his memories. When Susi got pregnant, they had been together for more than a year. Marriage had not been discussed. Susi spoke too often about getting away from the small town she was born in. A life she found suffocating. She had a lofty air about her as she tossed her hair and talked about going to America.

Father shakes his head, coming back to us. He looks over at me.

"Ach, your mother wanted so much more than I could give her. I didn't think I would ever be able to make her happy; she had too many dreams, your mother did. But I knew the right thing for everyone was that we become a family. I asked her to marry me. Of course, she immediately spat out no, and told me I could have no part of your upbringing. You know the rest; how I had to give up my rights. It was an incredibly sad time."

A difficult birth left Susi weak and dazed, bedridden in the hospital. Weeks went by before she recuperated enough to go back to her job as a waitress in Frankfurt. Here she met a French woman who needed one more girl for her dance troupe before taking off for the Middle East. Susi had several years of ballet lessons as a child and the cancan was easy enough to learn. She would leave me behind with Oma. I was five months old.

For five years my mother dressed in fabulous costumes, performed in supper clubs and lived in exotic places: Greece, Egypt, Lebanon, Iraq, and finally Turkey, where she met my stepfather. They came back to Germany, and she broke the news to my father that she was getting married to an Army Officer. He was going to adopt me.

Susi was on her way to America.

"Every German girl wanted to snag an American soldier—they were the ones who swaggered in the streets, gave cigarettes to the women, and chocolate bars to the children. Promises! Oh, did they make promises. Girls hung on the arms of young soldiers, hoping for marriage and a voyage to the land that had everything."

He shifts uncomfortably and sighs. Here are more memories he didn't want to revisit. Afternoon sun filters through the lace curtains behind him, his face is in silhouette. I glance at Michael, hoping, needing him to say something witty, but he remains mute. Father shakes his head, his face clears. He smiles with misty eyes as he rises and heads to the cabinets again, finds another photo album to put in my lap.

Here I am, page after page. Two groups of photos: at age three and then at five. I will find out they were taken during hard-won visits he negotiated with Oma while Mom was away. In the first group, I'm laughing at the camera and dressed to dazzle, in a plaid jumper and argyle leggings, holding a porcelain doll with perfect bud lips and a cloud of dark hair. I'm wearing round pink glasses, and my lace-up booties would be considered a find in any vintage store today. In the latter group, I have a pixie haircut and show off a scooter with stainless steel wheels. A huge grin highlights missing front teeth.

I cannot conjure up a single image of these times.

Memory. What is it exactly? Our senses compel impressions on us that become perceptions. Flashbulb memories, created from times of great emotional impact, constitute our earliest memories, good or bad. Long term memories are created by the successful storage and conversion of events. However, our brain decides what to remember. It can just as easily kick memories into the subconscious. Imagine yourself as a five-year-old, a day spent with a man who, you are told—or perhaps not—is your father. But he is not a part of your daily life. Your child's brain decides it may be best to forget.

Other days, you are told you have a mother, but you have no sense of her touch or smell or smile. Your life revolves around Oma, a woman who cares for you lovingly, but she moves slowly. You can outrun her when she shouts in frustration at another damn thing you've done. You know you are a hardship, so you hide in the musty cellar, or the dusty attic, whispering to yourself and listening intently for reassurances before you make your way back into the kitchen, head hanging. Tired arms reach out and enfold your skinny body with a sigh. Every small thing about her your child's brain wants to remember.

In these photos, I see a happy child, a loved child. How could I have forgotten?

Father pushes a DVD into the player. Scenes of my childhood converted from an old 8-millimeter film begin to play. I see Oma: blonde, slim, and looking younger than I remembered, smiling and leaning on a stone wall. There is another woman, large and imposing, laughing. It is Father's sister who's there with her daughter, a young teen with a dark bob and confident air.

The scrawny five-year-old in the video is flush with all the attention she's receiving. She rides her scooter with the stainless-steel rims around and around a small courtyard. She drops it and runs over to pick up a hula-hoop, excited and confident as it becomes a whirl around her skinny waist, then around her stick arms, and finally, around a strong and agile neck, the hoop huge but obedient. The camera pans out to show her admirers.

I watch in amazement, moved beyond words that he had kept it all these years.

The last scene in the home movie is five-year-old me at the zoo with my father and his new girlfriend, Anni, the woman to whom he is now married. She's out running errands today. When the video stops, Father asks if he can take my picture. Chuckling, he says he can't wait to let Anni know who visited him. He takes us to the long hallway wall covered in photos and points out a petite woman with short dark hair, a warm smile, and a direct gaze.

He proudly points to pictures of his handsome grandson Niklas, who is now sixteen, in various stages of growing up. I see pictures of my half-brother—also named Michael—and look for a resemblance, deciding he looks very much like a younger Walter. Again, it's the eyes that we all have in common, that crinkle up and almost disappear when we smile. I ask if my brother knows about me. Father says no, but he will soon; we'll all get together and have a family day. He rubs his hands in anticipation, then enfolds me in a tight hug.

As we climb into the car to drive back to Michael's home, Father stands in the parking lot and waves us down the road. Michael and I look at each other, wide-eyed at the afternoon's events. We sigh a collective sigh together.

"Oh, Michael! I can't even believe this has happened. A lifetime of wondering and wanting all came together in the last two hours. And he's healthy! His mind is sharp, too. I can't wait to sit down with him and learn about his life. And I have a new brother! Now what?"

Michael glances at me sideways.

"Well, his son might not be so happy to find out about you. And maybe Walter's wife won't be so happy about you showing up. Your father might have to work on his family for a while. We'll have to wait and see how it goes."

I fall silent. And think about the reaction from my unknown half-brother. At this stage in his life, he may not welcome me with open arms. He may see me as an intruder. He will certainly wonder why I show up now, when everyone is either in or approaching their golden years. A good time to hash things out would have been many years ago, when we all had more stamina and were probably more open-minded. Maybe.

I lean back in the seat and allow imagination to take me on a roller-coaster of scenarios, none of them good. But by the time we reach Michael's, I'm bursting with joy again and can't wait to rush in the house to call my husband and son with the news.

The Day After

Journal
June 2016

I always felt that my mother loved me grudgingly, as if love was something she could control by degrees. It wasn't until my son was born that I understood the power of uncontrollable love, when one's chest becomes a large bubble of warmth and joy, one's heart soft and pliable. The birth was difficult, and Jay was born via last-minute Cesarean. I demanded to be awake for it as we were rushed from the birthing room to the OR, my husband trotting beside the hospital bed. After my insides had been pulled open for what felt like an eternity, after my baby's squall pierced the heavy antiseptic air, after his acceptable Apgar score was shouted across the room, relief and love flooded me. For three days we snuggled in a hospital bed and stared at each other, the outside world unknown and uncared about. I was in a vacuum of security and acceptance. I knew I would never be alone again. I also knew my life was not my own anymore. To give someone unconditional love is an act of fearlessness that dwells deep in your heart and becomes a part of your soul.

I believe my father experienced a similar transformation many years ago. His acceptance when I showed up at his door unannounced was simply his heart remembering. I had spent much of life with my heart closed, to protect myself from an unmet yearning for unconditional love. I built walls and hid inside them, to guard against pain. When the possibility of pain got too close, I could harden my defenses and chase it away. I was afraid. Yesterday I was not. I knew my father loved me. Did I know this the last time I saw him, when I was five and we visited the Frankfurt Zoo?

I'm baffled at my lack of memories. Everything becomes a memory the instant we think it. The present exists only in the moment it occurs: a sequence of frames, each one a single image that blends into a whole to form perception. In doing research on childhood memory and childhood amnesia, I learned that language is key. Once a child can verbalize, events become more than internalized images, because she is able to attach meaning to them with words; she can talk about what happened. But events prior to language development can get lost, though they may return as flashes of images. For me, images in the garden appear, where I happily sat and watched Oma tend her strawberry patch while I popped berries into my mouth. I recall running around in the rich loam, Oma yelling at me to "watch where you plant your feet; if you're not careful you will get stuck and have to wait for harvest to be plucked."

Next, the stage at which a child realizes she is a unique and separate individual from her parents creates memories as she becomes the primary player. These are referred to as autobiographical episodes. Images that arise without an attached story are considered flashbulb memories, brought on by events with a strong emotional component. A deep need, one that left me feeling physically empty, is one such memory. When I sat for hours at the kitchen window willing a strange man to come to our door to claim me, I attached meaning to the yearning. I wanted a father to come and claim me. But why a father and not a mother? Perhaps because when my father came for a visit (some of the photos he showed me were clearly taken in front of our quadplex) I retained a memory of him walking down the sidewalk. But although I have other vivid memories from my childhood, I recognized none of the scenes in the home movie, where I show off the scooter and hula hoop.

Shortly after that home movie was made in 1960, my mother appeared in Oma's doorway, suitcases in hand, with a new father. Perhaps I felt I had to let go of one father to accept another and buried those memories. Familiar feelings of anger at Mom stab me, feelings I was able to suppress in her final years. Illness softened her; her frailty took away the power she had over me. We spoke the words *I love you* to each other after a lifetime of strife. My mother never seemed to know happiness. She struggled as a wife and as a mother not only to me but also to the children she gave Ted. To see the person she had been, happy and filled with hope, is poignant.

•

In a photo album Mom gave me for my fiftieth birthday are the photographs I should have seen many years earlier: a new mother proudly holding her infant daughter. Me as a baby at five months propped up next to a tree, squinting and smiling. On the back she had written: *mein kleiner Liebling*. My little darling. The photo was taken right before she left me at Oma's and departed with the dance troupe. For those first few months together, did we also cuddle and stare at each other? Mom never told me these stories, the ones I tell my son, of how his birth day was the best day of my life. She told me how depleted and empty she was after she gave birth. She told me this when I questioned the name on my birth certificate: Ursula. My father's choice, because she was too ill to provide the name she had already chosen: Madeleine.

The album has several pictures that were taken after I came to live with Mom and Ted in Frankfurt. Many are random poses, going down the stairs on my way outside to play, or sitting on the couch after washing my hair, a towel wrapped turban-like around my head. I don't remember these times. Recently, Jackie sent a photo she found while going through Mom's memorabilia. It was of an elaborate table setting, clearly a party. A Barbie doll cake sat in the middle of pastel colored paper plates, cups, and napkins, all on a colorful tablecloth. Once I saw it, I did remember. It was my seventh birthday, the first one we celebrated after we became a family. But I don't recall who came or what we did. Did we play games, like pin the tail on the donkey? Did other kids come or was it only family? I had wanted a Barbie doll desperately since I discovered her. Did I get her for this birthday? I seem to remember it was later, when I was almost old enough to not want her anymore.

Language was certainly a defining factor as I started at Frankfurt American School without a verbal understanding of what was happening around me. I heard only a babble of foreign words. By the time I remember school episodes in third grade, I had fallen in love with my new language and spent my free time reading books and writing stories. A foundation of identity.

Identity. This seemed to be a problem for me although I didn't recognize it at the time. I felt displaced, that I wasn't where I belonged. While I lived with Oma, I was her granddaughter, but I was missing the parents children initially identify with. Yet when my mother came home and offered me the father and family life I had so desired, it only added confusion.

Recently I ran across research titled *Identity Problems Related to an Absent Genetic Father.* Written by Dutch therapists, the study goes into detail about how children who do not know their biological fathers develop social problems such "as entering and maintaining close relationships, the feeling of not belonging, feelings of having little control over one's life and problems with making decisions in life." They posit that our self-image is comprised of many facets, but the formation begins in infancy. During this time, we see our parents as the markers of our traits in everything from looks to likes. If the father is absent, the child may assume the traits that did not come from the mother must have come from the absent father. In other words, she creates a fantasized image of the missing father to whom she attributes the differences between her and the mother. In theory, this creates a lack of completeness in herself.

Since I didn't know my mother until I was almost six, I basically lacked both reference points, both parents. Once I did live with her, I found my mother lacking: in love and affection, in being able to control her emotions, in any recognizable skill or talent that impressed my young and judgmental self. Mom refused to talk about my genetic father. Instead, she insisted Ted was the only father I needed to know. This was unacceptable to me. This felt wrong. I could not relate to my stepfather. He was remote. He was a disciplinarian.

Another stage where memories drop out are at the onset of puberty. Neurobiological processes essential during this time eject memories our brain decides are not crucial. Is it possible that I had retained some memories and at this stage let them go? During my teen years I was desperate to present myself as an American, obsessed with my looks, slouched and insolent as I imagined someone who is cool would be. After I began to drive, friends, school, and part-time work became my existence. I was a ghost who came home late at night and left early. Many nights were spent at friends' houses. At eighteen I moved out. As my psyche grappled with identity, how easily my mind could have shunted certain early memories, leaving holes in their place.

But I compare the memories I do have at ages four or five to my research. It is obvious there are more holes. I remember my grandmother, aunts, uncle, some cousins, even neighbors. But no father. Nor anyone from his family, including his niece, Brigitte, a sultry girl with a glorious chestnut bob. Here is the first flashbulb image: in one photo, she stands close behind me, a hand on each shoulder. She's fifteen and I'm five. We both offer a pout to the camera, share the same haircut and stance. The background is Father's homestead, the same courtyard where I ran circles with the red scooter. Judging from the photo and our identical hairstyles, style of dress, and expressions, we must have had a relationship; I was clearly trying to emulate her. Which makes me think I had been to Father's home more than once. But aside from a brief flash of knowing that I knew her, I don't remember her either.

My father was not a stranger when he appeared in front of me yesterday. I knew instantly who he was. As he did me. And somewhere was a connection from that dusty bin in my mind to the heart which prompted it to open, to accept this man I didn't know as the longed-for father. Beyond the pumping of blood from emotion and nerves, I felt the ease of *already* knowing him, of trusting him. But not remembrance. It is possible that Mom may have ranted, or quietly intoned, about my father when I was a child. Not understanding, but with a sense of their relationship being bad, I may have blocked images relating to him.

The challenge now is how I can fit into his life. How much can we communicate with each other about our lives, given the difference in languages? How much time will we spend together? Is it feasible to think I can visit for a few weeks or more? That we walk and talk and really get to know one another? Or will it be Christmas and birthday cards with an occasional dinner when I'm in Germany visiting my cousins? How will his son react when he learns he's not an only child? How will he respond to this secret out of nowhere?

Cousin Brigitte and Madeleine, circa 1960

So many questions remain to be answered. This journey has only just begun. I hope for the best, but I have created circumstances—the opening of old histories and wounds—much as Aunt Sieglinde did when she unleashed her secret.

Lebensborn e.V.

Neustadt
July 2016

As Michael and I plan our trip to Munich to hear Sieglinde's story, we take the afternoon to research *Lebensborn*, the Nazi program that mandated "genetically correct" coupling in order to populate the Third Reich. While the delicious smells of Sicilian chicken waft around us, we settle in at Michael's kitchen table with our respective laptops and type the word into our search engines. Up pop multiple pages related to the subject. Turns out several movies had been produced dealing with the baby-making program, and the experiments based on eugenics. But they were typical Hollywood: exaggerated and dramatic. We find more articles: *Lebensborn: Secret Nazi Breeding Program*; *The Woman Who Gave Birth for Hitler*; *Himmler's Children*. There is even an interactive video game that allows players to "raise" a Lebensborn child. Called *My Child Lebensborn*, a player can take the role of a parent who has adopted a child from a program participant and agreed to raise it in the proper German way.

Michael looks shell-shocked. I'm nauseated. Our aunt has been living with this secret for forty-six years. Now my cousins and I have to come to some kind of reckoning. Some kind of acceptance. I jot down notes and compile the facts that I consider essential and viable.

•

Lebensborn e.V. (Lebensborn Eingetragener Verein) became an official registered organization on December 12, 1935. Translation: fount of life. (A fount can be a spring, a source. It can also be the vessel which gives forth something, in this case children.) Germany's birth rate had been in a steep decline for decades. WWI had taken its toll on young available men. The economy was in tatters, inflation was out of control and food was scarce. Abortions were estimated to have reached eight hundred thousand in the inter-war years before 1935. Motherhood seemed to be the least of people's concerns. Hitler needed soldiers. Heinrich Luitpold Himmler provided a solution. One of the most powerful men in the Nazi party, he created the program to help Hitler reach a goal of one hundred and twenty million pure Aryan citizens for the Third Reich.

I keep digging, into history and the Aryans. I wonder what would have happened had Hitler not met Himmler. Yes, the Jews would still have been persecuted, but what of the Lebensborn program; would that still have come to be? The heartbreak, guilt, and displaced identities of thousands of "genetically superior" children who were born or kidnapped to fit a crazy man's ideal. It boggles my mind.

Fascinated with the concept of a superior race, Himmler drew his beliefs from the works of Joseph Arthur Gobineau, a French aristocrat, diplomat, and novelist in the nineteenth century. Gobineau had developed a flawed theory of an Aryan master race. In a 1,400-page manuscript, *An Essay on the Inequality of the Human Race,* he posited that aristocrats were superior genetically to commoners. He cited ancient Hindu scriptures declaring the highest caste to be descendants of the Aryans. This was, however, a self-designation of the noble class during the Vedic age of 1500-500 BCE, when the oldest scriptures of Hinduism were composed. Misinterpretation of history allowed Gobineau to adopt this term as a racial category and apply it to the northern Europeans who migrated across the world.

Gobineau screwed up.

The perfect Aryan specimen. Michael and I chuckle as we read this. The lack of Aryan characteristics is obvious in Hitler and his closest henchmen. Instead of tall, blond Teutonic specimens, they were dark-haired men of ordinary stature, who surrounded themselves with an ideal they could not come close to: the elite men of the Schutzstaffel, or SS.

Himmler, *Reichsführer* of the Schutzstaffel, and Hitler's second in command, had developed the SS from a 290-man battalion in 1929 to a million-strong paramilitary unit by the time the war ended in May of 1945. Each man was painstakingly vetted for looks, strength, intelligence, and purity of blood—i.e., no Jewish or other dubious ancestry—going back several generations. Initially, programs of Lebensborn simply encouraged SS families to have more children, using incentives such as money and recognition. The program expanded to all Germans, and a gold Mother's Cross was awarded to families with eight children or more, to be proudly displayed in a window for all to see.

I thought about my Oma and how motherhoood had seemed to come so easily to her. I remembered the photos of her through the years posing with her children. She was always dressed to the nines, with heels to accentuate her willowy stature and her blonde hair in an upsweep topped by a stylish hat. Her girls grouped around her, in perfectly ironed pinafores, hair neatly combed and held in place with ribbons and barrettes. She could have been a postergirl for the ideal Third Reich mother.

Over time, the program expanded even more. SS officers were encouraged to couple with young women, in or out of wedlock, who fit the Aryan ideal of blonde hair, blue eyes, no genetic disorders and a clean bloodline. By 1939, SS participation in Lebensborn was mandatory, a quiet but undisputable order given along with deployment. Himmler stated, "Should we succeed in establishing this Nordic race, and from this seedbed produce a race of two hundred million, then the world will belong to us."

•

I wondered how Katharina was approached, what words were used to encourage her participation. She was living in Deggendorf at the time, a twenty-six-year-old woman with three small children and a husband dedicated to Hitler's Army. He was gone most of the time. *Was* Katharina approached, or did she volunteer? Did she lay with one man, or was it several? To understand the allure to the young women willing to participate, one has to understand the Nazi propaganda machine.

I found several articles online about a young woman devoted to having children for the Reich. Beginning in 1936, it was compulsory for girls aged ten and up to join the Bund Deutscher Mädel: the BDM, or League of German Girls. Their young minds were indoctrinated to serve Hitler and the Third Reich. Brainwashed to proudly offer themselves for their country. In the few testimonies available, what comes across is not only a distorted devotion to Germany, but also to Hitler the man.

Eighteen-year-old Hildegard Trutz was at a loss at the end of her schooling of how to contribute to Hitler's vision. She shared her concerns with a BDM leader who quietly suggested she create a child for the Führer; what Hitler needed most was racially pure stock. Hildegard was given the address of a maternity home near the Tegernsee in south Bavaria called Hochland, an old castle that housed about forty girls. Hildegard admits she was wildly excited not only at the prospect of mating with a good-looking SS officer and being pampered, but also at being able to give the Führer something he valued.

I think back on my twenties and remember how impressionable I was. How I floundered, questioning my place in the world. My purpose. A young woman, especially one with limited prospects, could easily convince herself she was doing something noble. Propaganda was everywhere: in order for Germany to claim its elite place in the world, all must do their part.

The first official Lebensborn maternity home, *Heim Hochland*, was located in tiny Steinhoring, just outside of Munich. The four-story building, reminiscent of a chalet, offered a safe place for single women to have their children without stigma. Regardless of nationalistic fervor, sex out of wedlock was still taboo with the older generation. Testimonies from women reveal they kept their condition a secret and invented an excuse, such as work or a study program, to leave their hometowns.

Female participants had to submit to physical examinations and provide documentation of ethnic purity going back several generations. Faces were measured: the distance between eyes, eye size in relation to the eyebrows, and the nose in relation to the mouth. The women resided in private rooms with costly furnishings looted from Jewish homes. Clothes and toiletries were provided, delicious meals served.

Adoption services placed their children into "proper" German families. But first, the babies were "baptized" in an elaborate ceremony under a Swastika emblem with an SS dagger held over their heads. The photos Michael and I found online depicting this ceremony are frightening in their formality and pomp. The children's lives were given to Hitler. Their value was in blood.

One photo in particular broke my heart: strollers lined up in a long row, outside in the bright sunshine. Nannies in crisp uniforms stand behind each one, smiling benignly at a tiny, wrapped bundle with a fluff of blonde hair. These are the children who would grow up in a shroud of silence as to their beginnings. These are the children who would probably feel the sense of displacement as they grew up in families—some prominent, some mainstream—who had a secret to endure for the rest of their lives.

It is estimated that at least 8,000 children were officially born under Lebensborn in Germany, far short of Himmler's original goal. (I have read sources that claim one hundred and twenty million and two hundred million. Either way, the program was considered a failure). As the war progressed, and the Nazi machine moved into other countries, the program continued, especially in Scandinavia. Viking blood was considered superior. Estimates place up to 12,000 children born in Norway alone. Horror stories abound. Many of the Norwegian women who gave birth to "German bastards" were sent to Norwegian concentration camps after the war. Their children were placed in asylums. Others were sometimes taken in by foster families and mistreated. One woman told about being chained in the yard with the dog.

The program added another unimaginable component: kidnapping. "Genetically correct" children were snatched from their families in occupied countries. Many were taken in full view of their parents. Others were told their families had given them up or had died. They were then categorized into three groups: those who met all criteria were labelled highly desirable and placed with German families; those who were deemed acceptable were placed into orphanages for more testing; and those who were deemed unwanted after all, were sent to work camps or exterminated.

How inhumane for these families to have had their children snatched away. How traumatic for those children who were handed to new families to grow up under the mantle of lies. Worse yet, for those who were executed simply because their eyes were set too close together or because their nose was a half-inch too long. As we read this, Michael and I look closely at each other and realize neither one of us would have passed muster.

In 2006, the story broke in Germany and Britain that a group of thirty Lebensborn children met in the small farming town of Wenigerode in Eastern Germany. The meeting was monickered Lebensspuren (Traces of Life). They came together as a self-help group organized by Georg Lilienthal, a German historian who, after extensive research, published a book in 1985 titled *Der Lebensborn e.V.* He writes: "After the Second World War, the Lebensborn e.V. (a registered association) was long considered one of the most mysterious institutions of the National Socialist regime. That its secret could be successfully concealed under the Third Reich attracted a great deal of public curiosity after 1945. The public only learned of its existence during the Nuremberg Trials …"

•

The number of lives impacted by Lebensborn, either directly or indirectly, will never be known. Like my grandmother, women who participated paid a high price. Guilt, broken homes, and the burden of keeping a secret that so deeply affected their children. Sieglinde knew instinctively that she was different, a common feeling expressed by the children who met in the Lebensspuren group.

It is foolish to assume that the program was only used officially. An officer did not need stamped and documented paperwork to convince a desirable woman to share her bed and to do her duty for the Führer. It was wartime. With all able-bodied men deployed, women struggled alone to raise their families. Every day was an uncertainty. In places such as Montabaur, a strategic location with garrisons close to Frankfurt, enlisted men and officers flooded the small town. All goods were rationed, at least for the common citizenry. If an officer showed up with a ham, a little precious coffee, or maybe even a cord of wood for the stove … well. Or perhaps a murmur reminded a pretty young hausfrau that her husband may also be contributing to the Führer's need. And yet, after the Third Reich imploded, they kept their secrets out of shame and humiliation. Like my Oma.

Sieglinde's Story

Munich
July 2016

Michael, Thomas, and I settle ourselves around the kitchen table, fortified with food and drink for what we know will be a long night. My aunt sits down, a sheaf of paperwork in her hands. Her notes: her father's name and address, his daughter's name. Address, occupation. A confirmation letter from the Red Cross who had helped her in her search, as they helped so many other children with questions about their fathers or lost families. All written in the shorthand Sieglinde learned as a young woman, and still uses to write her journals. Her usually animated face looks drawn and apprehensive. She's had to dwell on the past to put together the words she will tell us.

•

I always felt like I didn't belong. My earliest memories are about looking at my three older sisters and feeling very different. Susi, Gunda, and Erika had dark hair and sharp features, their blue eyes deep-set and intense. They looked like their father, the man I believed had also been my father. To me, they seemed like three peas in a pod. I was blonde with softer features, larger eyes. When I was old enough to understand these things, I expected Mutti to tell me I was adopted.

I was eight when Mutti became pregnant with Hans Herbert. By then I knew that a father made babies. I got very excited when I realized she would have another baby and ran to ask her who our father was. She got angry and told me I was her child. Her child! I guess we didn't need a father. And I realized this was a secret between us. From that point on I felt close to my mother. I slept in the main bedroom with her while the others slept in the attic. I felt special.

One day—I might have been at the bakery for some day-old rolls—I heard whispering from two women. I turned to look at them and they gave me a hard look back. Even then I knew people talked about our family, especially the old women in their worn-out housedresses and scornful eyes. I ran all the way home, feeling afraid and sad. And angry. Mutti cleaned houses, and repaired the soldiers' laundry so that we could eat. She had to work hard every day and was always tired and had forgotten how to smile.

Maddie, your mother Susi, as the oldest, was responsible for helping to clean the house and wash our clothes. In my earliest memories she was the little mother. It was hard for her. She was thin, and sick a lot. But she didn't have a choice. As poor as we were, Mutti wanted a spotless home and for her children to be clean and neatly dressed. Because Mutti worked every day, the resposibility fell on Susi. When this didn't happen, Mutti pulled out a hickory switch and flailed away at bare legs, mostly Susi's. I know now that she walked the edge, hid things about her life from us. And how important it was to her to give the impression of family.

I asked her again and again about a father. Fathers were a mystery. And, oh, how I wanted one! But I never got an answer, only hard looks.

Right after Hans Herbert was born, Mutti had to have an operation. Christel, the youngest girl, had been flouncing around her while she was breastfeeding newborn Hansi and accidentally elbowed Mutti's breast. Or maybe she fell into it and used her elbow to push herself away. Whatever happened, one of Mutti's milk ducts got infected, some kind of abscess that had to be cut out. The first time, the doctor botched it and it had to be done again. This left Mutti depleted. She sent for her sister, my Aunt Susanne, to help out for a while. Susanne was a nun. I loved having her there. She was a happy person and brought happiness into our home.

She took us wandering into the woods and meadows. We hiked and sang and picked berries and wildflowers. One day she pointed to the sky—it was clear and a true sky blue—and said God must be so happy today, because he had given us a perfect day. She sat down next to me in the grass and took my small hands in hers. She looked at me very intently and asked if I knew about Jesus. I shook my head. Then my beloved aunt told me something that changed my life: she told me there was a Father in heaven who loved me dearly and wished all good things for me. If I dedicated myself to him, he would always be with me. I didn't have to worry about things; I just needed to raise my hands and ask for help.

Oh! How amazed I was. That day I gave myself to Jesus and never looked back. And He has always been there for me, guiding me.

I had a Father. And He loved me.

•

For little Sieglinde Helene, that day provided a revelation: a Father for all children, a harbor of love and safety that had been missing. One she always remembered a yearning for. Now she could carry her father in her heart and never be without him. For the child who felt misplaced, this was the perfect answer. As she grew, so did her faith, until it was the one defining factor in everything she did. The perfect answer to not having a father became having one that was with her always, who guided when she needed guidance and who comforted when she needed comforting. She always asked herself if this was the way God wanted her to live. She says that although she considered monastic life, she felt that wasn't what God wanted from her. He needed her light to shine forth in other ways.

•

Our life was so hard. We all had to work. When I was only six, I got up with Mutti while it was still dark, to help her deliver newspapers on her bicycle. I sat on the handlebars and threw the papers into the driveways. When we were done, she would ride the bike up the hill to the Joseph-Kehrein Schule. I would jump off the handlebars and go to classes until early afternoon, then walk to a home, where I was a mother's help for three small children. The youngest was just seven weeks old. In the evenings Mutti would pick me up from there to help clean offices in town. This was exciting for me because I became fascinated by the typewriter. I decided right then that I wanted to learn how to work in an office. Mutti would yell at me because I dawdled around the machines, goggle-eyed, trying to figure out how they worked.

We all cleaned. Even little Christel, at three, would help dust. Our school had been converted to a hospital by that time. So we worked. And we waited for the war to end. Every day I woke up hoping to hear that the war was over, that our soldiers would come home. Maybe a father would show up. In the winter it was hard to get food, especially in the last year of the war. Sometimes Mutti had to take potato peelings from the houses she cleaned, to make soup. We were thankful to have an evening meal and our mother was thankful to go to bed.

Susi helped us kids get into bed at night. Although we were always tired, it was a time of anxiety, a time to wait for the sirens. By the end of the war, it happened most nights. We were too close to Frankfurt. Mostly the planes flew over, but Montabaur also had garrisons for the army. Our train station was blown up, but luckily not much else.

We all kept a small bundle of clothes and soap by our bed. When the sirens went off, we grabbed our bundles and scampered down the hill to the bunker across the river. Everything was blacked out, so we ran by the light of the moon. After a while, we knew the way so well we could have done it with our eyes closed. But we had to be fast, or the door would be shut. Our neighborhood gathered there and we would sit in the dark to wait until the all clear sounded. Sometimes it was hours.

•

Imagine this as a way of life. Was it better to be a child, to not yet understand how wrong it is to have to live this way? To be able to accept things as they needed to be rather than how they should be? As an adult, do you look back on this time as one of trauma or as one that simply was? Oma often stayed behind, down in the dank cellar, rocking little Christel back to sleep and praying that the bombs hit other targets, far away from this town and this home. Then later, she may have felt she couldn't make it to the bunker in time, heavy with Hansi in her womb. In early 1945 the Allied bombers flew over night after night.

By now, Allied foot patrols had penetrated German borders. By now, the world was beginning to understand the horrors hidden in the concentration camps. By now, the shining myth of the Thousand Year Reich was disintegrating.

•

There were nights I would wake up to someone pounding on the door. The officers came around for "bed check," making sure everyone was inside for curfew. Now I know the soldiers went to the pretty women with no men in the house. There were other places where soldiers met with girls, an inn here in town. One time I overheard three young women outside a store, laughing and betting on the sex of the babies they would make. They were excited and commented on the good looks of their partners, how beautiful the children would be. I was too young to know then that they were referring to what was called freiheit (the freedom) that allowed them to have sex outside of marriage for the sake of the Reich. I was confused but understood that they were talking about fathers. I didn't know then that I was one of those freedom babies.

One night—I'm really not sure when, because my memory is so hazy. I was still very young. I woke up because I heard what sounded like a scream. When I wandered into the kitchen, I saw Mutti on the big farmhouse table on her back. Other people were around her, over her. There was a lot of blood. Red blood everywhere. On Mutti, on the table. Crimson rags piled up. I started screaming. Someone grabbed me and took me upstairs to the attic bedroom, to Christel's room. I kept asking if Mutti was dying. No, no, she would be fine. Mutti spent a few days in her bed. Now I know she had an abortion that night. Mutti was already in her mid-thirties, a still young woman with too many children. I guess she didn't want anymore.

I don't know about the fathers of Christel and Hans Herbert. Christel thinks her father was a shoemaker in civilian life, but I don't know what he did as a soldier. Hans Herbert's father might have been a tailor who sewed uniforms. I heard that he was recovering from a war injury of some kind. I also heard that he was Austrian, but who knows.

•

I picked up on an underlying note of doubt that Katharina was ever threatened. The possibility that she was simply promiscuous hung in the air. Sieglinde's story, and the discovery of Lebensborn within our family, is enough to send Germans scurrying for cover. Is it easier to believe that the lovely Katharina enjoyed extra-marital relations, or that she was coerced? The extra attic room, the one that wasn't used for a bedroom, was used to house soldiers at different times. Perhaps they were recuperating from injuries, perhaps they were traveling between stations. We don't know what happened in that attic room. We do know what Sieglinde has told us, from the information she was able to get.

•

My father was a doctor who worked with prosthetics. I'll never forget the day Mutti finally told me. She had come to Sulzbach to visit me; I was very pregnant with my youngest. After I married Schorsh, Mutti and I didn't see each other much. The children came and I was busy being a mother and wife. We sat in the kitchen and finally I asked her again, very strongly, I demanded to know who my real father was. She sat and shook her head in refusal. Her lips were pressed into a thin line, as if she was afraid words would jump out. Finally she got up and headed to the door, to leave without even saying good-bye. She stopped short, and over her shoulder she told me his name, his birthdate and the town he was from. She told me more, but my mind was reeling. I do remember she said she was approached by the Nazis while living in Deggendorf. There may have been as many as eight other women who were also involved in the program in that town. I ran back into the kitchen to write everything down. Then she left. I never saw her again. In one year she would be dead from a heart condition.

I was able to look up an address for my father. People don't move around much and I thought there was a good chance he may still live there. But he had moved to a town nearby. The people who lived in his old place told me they knew him, his wife, and his daughter. That he came back to his old town every few weeks to have a beer or two with friends. In fact, they were expecting him that weekend. At first I planned to come back also and confront him, but I got very nervous and didn't. Afraid. That's what I was. Afraid he would reject me. I let it go for a few years. I wasn't brave enough. I convinced myself it was enough to finally know about him.

•

Here I sit up, jolted by this similarity in our stories. Often I have asked myself why I didn't pursue finding my father. Intense interest in him when I was a teen faded with marriage and life. Over and over I told myself it wasn't so important to know my father. But underlying the excuses was simply fear. The thought of outright rejection was terrifying. In Sieglinde's case, the chance of rejection may have felt like a certainty, given the circumstances. And perhaps the fact that he may have been a monster.

•

Eventually I wrote him a letter and told him I was his daughter. I told him about my life, as a mother, and about my faith. That I hoped he had a good life and wished him well. I didn't hear back. Finally I got up the courage to go to his house. His wife answered the door. I stood tall, looked her in the eyes and said I was there to meet my father. She must have read the letter, because her face filled with hatred and she spit out, "He did what he was told to do. Go away from here, you have no part in our family." And the door slammed. I left. Later, I learned from his old neighbors that he had died.

I regret not trying to meet him all those years ago. I regret my lack of courage.

Not long after, I received a call from the daughter's son. In going through some old papers he found the letter I had written to his grandfather. He asked if I wanted a photo. Of course I did! I have it hanging in my office. At least I would know what he looked like.

My father is buried in Amberg where his family is from. I was able to find his grave. I sat down in front of it and cried and cried. I shook my fist and railed against what he had done, the coldness of it all. But ultimately, I forgave him. And when I did, I immediately felt a peace in my heart. It was what God wanted from me. I wouldn't be here if he hadn't lay with Mutti. I only wish he could have been a part of our lives.

•

Did my grandmother confess because she knew she was dying? Or was she simply tired of the lies? Perhaps the shame of the burden seem too large to carry that afternoon as she sat in Sieglinde's kitchen, her long-limbed torso now heavy with bloat from congestive heart failure, her blonde hair now silver. How often did she think about those knocks on the door late at night, the handsome and powerful men who guided her to her bed? Did they whisper in her ear, did they bring gifts, did they make her feel special? Or did they demand she lie down to do her "duty?" I think back to the wedding photo, the pure joy in Katharina's face as she leans into her new husband. The question arises: what happened just four short years later?

•

Lebensborn killed Mutti's husband Felix, the man I was told was my father. He was a soldier and loyal to the cause but he couldn't accept his wife sleeping with other men, not even for The Third Reich. Twice he came home from the war, and twice he found his wife pregnant.

It almost killed me, too.

For two years, Felix worked in Montabaur, overseeing the building of homes for the Army, including his own. This was during the time Mutti and the first three girls lived in Deggendorf. When their home was finished, he sent for them and found his wife ready to give birth. To me. He told her I couldn't be his; the timing was off. He became furious and beat her, kicking her in the belly. He locked her in the bathroom and told her to flush the baby down the toilet. Me … I was almost flushed down the toilet!

I found all this out at Mutti's funeral. Our old neighbors told me; they were the ones who saved her. They lived behind her in the quadplex and heard her screaming. They said they sneaked food to her through the window, while Felix, a crazed man, guarded the front door. I don't know who took care of the other children. I guess Felix did. They must have been so frightened! Felix was a madman, the neighbors told me. But somehow, after a few days, Mutti was able to convince him that I was his. She begged him to believe her. But soon he had to leave again. The war had officially started. It may have been during this time that he also took up with another woman in town, but he still provided for his family. I guess he came and went. He had his doubts. The trust was broken.

A few years later, he came home from a tour to find Mutti pregnant again, this time with Christel. He became incensed. He railed against Hitler; he railed against the soldiers who tended to women while their husbands were off fighting the war. Soon after, Felix was sent on what was called a Himmelfahrt—a ride to heaven—which meant he was put on the frontlines to die. We're not sure where exactly. While there, he put a gun to his temple, or so we were told. His grave is probably a mass grave. Mutti tried to collect his pension, but she wasn't able to. She went to the army offices in town many times. I used to go with her. But they told her that because he killed himself, he was a disgrace, a traitor. So no pension.

Things were really hard for our family. It was especially bad after the war. We all became apprentices after we finished our basic schooling at fourteen. I was taken in by the Deaconess Home where my Aunt Susanne was a nun. There I trained in clerical work. Finally I got to use all the office equipment I so loved when I was a little girl. I also had a warm bed and plenty of food. I was still there at nineteen, when I met my future husband. Schorsh came roaring into town on his motorcycle. I remember him pulling up, windswept and wearing sunglasses. I fell madly in love and became a wife and mother. I made a new life for myself and created my own history. I didn't know then that I would one day search for my father and find out that I was a baby created for the Führer.

After the Truth

Munich
July 2016

Aunt Sieglinde has gone off to bed. In her typical efficient manner, she gathered her notes together, thumped them on the table for good measure and headed upstairs. No doubt to sleep soundly. I sit and stare at my cousins Michael and Thomas. Like me, they are glassy-eyed and stunned. We are sprawled at Thomas' kitchen table, which is littered with empty cookie wrappers, half-full glasses of water and a bit of Grauburgunder wine. I reach for the bottle and empty it into my glass. Thomas struggles to his feet, plods down winding stairs to the cellar for another.

"I never knew my grandmother Katharina," Thomas confesses as he returns and uncorks the bottle. "I have one clear memory of her. She came to our house in Sulzbach and sat in our kitchen with a cigarette, smoke drifting up in front of her face. I think I only remember this because she was allowed to smoke in our house, which was unheard of. This must have been the time she confessed to my mother."

He pours two fingers of wine all around. We pick up our glasses and toss it down, like pungent whiskey instead of the dry fruitiness we all complimented at first sip hours ago when Sieglinde's story began. Although I remembered hearing stories about genetic testing, Goering's experiments on prisoners—many on children—and about

Hitler's obsession with a superior race, I had never bothered to look for details. Shame always crept in. It felt like a blight on my heritage.

"Now what?" I mumble at Michael. He shrugs, blows out a long breath. Runs shaky fingers through his cropped hair, leaving a point. An exclamation mark. Perfect. Thomas's lanky frame is sprawled as he stares up at the ceiling, imagining who knows what.

Nothing eases this mind-obsession now: my beloved Oma waiting for a late-night knock on her door, the bedcovers laid back. I suddenly remember a comment I overheard my mother say right after Katharina's death. I was sixteen, hovering in the hallway in our Florida home while she spoke on the phone to one of her siblings in Germany. She was asking about her mother's paperwork and was told it had all been thrown out by Hans Herbert, her brother. Was she thinking about official Lebensborn paperwork? Had she known more about her mother's actions than she ever let on? As the oldest, she would have been the one to notice surreptitious comings and goings and understood enough.

Yet, after the phone call she made a vague comment that made my scalp prickle and my stomach sour. At the time, I hated my mother for saying the words she did, but now I decide it was fine if my grandmother "opened her legs to any man that paid her attention." At least that meant she gave herself willingly.

•

I stare at the family portrait in my old album and now understand the truth of what I see.

Here they are, six fatherless children and the spouseless mother, all dressed up. The photo was probably taken in 1948 in a photographer's studio. My beloved grandmother sits in an upholstered chair, in a black high-necked dress and a simple long chain as adornment. Her hands are folded in her lap. A chaste Madonna. Her tired and worldly eyes are a contrast to the innocent anticipation in her wedding photo, the husband she lovingly leaned into, now many years dead. Did she now sleep alone in her bed? Was she relieved? No more knocks on the door late at night; no more lonely births. She is the resigned and tired mother, her only purpose in life to finish raising her family alone.

Heartbreaking.

Now it's easy for me to see the differences in paternity. The three oldest are sharp-beaked and intense, like their one father. The younger three are blonde and striking, as their three fathers may have been, although it would be easy to say they take after their mother. They are, after all, the desired combination demanded by nationalistic furor, part of the imagined Aryan supremacy foolishly based on looks.

When I first saw the photo many years ago, I didn't know the paternal secrets. At that time, I wondered at the solemn faces, at the differences in appearance. Now I wonder if this photo was taken as Katharina's determined documentation of a family, no man necessary, only a Herz einer Mutter, a mother's heart of love. It is my aunt's confession that gives me the knowledge of what I now see. In the photo Sieglinde stands close to Katharina, relaxed and smiling, her eyes engaging with the camera. She will grow up to be tall and strong and healthy and smart and self-assured.

Left to right: Christel, Erika, Gunda, Hans Herbert sitting on Susi's lap, Sieglinde, Katharina. Circa 1948

Family Day

Bad Nauheim
July 2016

Oh no, we're five minutes late. I glance at Michael and know he's thinking the same, this cousin who shares my penchant for never arriving early. My eighty-nine-year-old father is pacing the side-walk in front of the apartment complex where he and his wife live. I can't miss his ramrod bearing as we drive up the hill: three steps up, three steps back; a pirouette as he peers around, maybe thinking we sneaked past and are already parked.

My chest tightens as I whisper "What is he doing? Did something happen? Have they changed their mind?" A bit frantic now.

Michael grins. "No, I think he's going to help us park. Typical German of his generation, he wants to conduct things the best way. It also may be why it took a while to hear from him. Everything had to be in order. You'll see."

We pull up next to him with a smile and a wave. He looks relieved, and without a word or smile turns on his heels and marches toward a side street, arm up like a flag. He guides us into a parking spot in front of a daycare.

"It's okay to park here on the weekends, they're closed," he informs us as Michael pulls up and we get out. "All the parking spaces for the apartment are assigned and I didn't want you to try and park in the street."

Now comes a quick hug for me, a handshake for Michael. Father's anxious face relaxes into a grin. Eyes disappear behind cheekbones, mustache quivers.

"The others are waiting for us at the restaurant," he says.

Michael looks alarmed. "Are we very late?"

"No, no. I thought it would be best if we weren't all here waiting for you." Father takes off and we scramble to catch up. "We'll walk down; it's just a few blocks."

The restaurant is built on the grounds of a natural spring touted as a life elixir. It's long and spacious, with a wall of windows looking out over the terrace. We walk in and follow my father to a table filled with people who are watching us.

Uh, oh. They don't look happy, my mind whispers.

Father stops in front of the table and loudly announces: "This is my daughter; let's welcome her."

His arm is out as he presents me. His voice is firm and commanding, a voice I will get to know well and love for its unambiguity. But for now, I'm painfully on display. A flush begins at my neck. My cousin stands next to me. Faces stare up at us. Polite and curious faces. *They are trying to make the best of an awkward situation. Be charming. You can do this.* What I really want is an excuse to leave. I have no place here in this family. Why, oh why, did I even think they would want to meet me? I've lived with the knowledge of having an unknown father for an entire life. My brother and his family have only known about the bastard child for a few weeks now. I'm tainted before I ever open my mouth. Panic fills me.

As a middle-aged man rises from the table and reaches out his hand, Father states "This is your sister." My brother is ten years younger than me. His face is carefully pleasant, his greeting brief and polite. Introductions and handshakes go round: fifteen-year-old grandson Niklas; Bettina, my brother's wife; and Anni, Father's wife of fifty-five years. I'm seated between the two Michaels, with Father across from me. He alone looks confident and clearly delighted.

I smile and nod at everyone. They smile and nod back, then quickly look away. It's a warm day; the doors are open. A tiny rivulet of sweat on the back of my neck trickles between scrunched shoulder blades. My confidence is already shaken by the number of days since we rang my father's doorbell. Nineteen of them. Two and half weeks. I imagined many conversations, and many silences, during this time. Now I think I was probably right. If I had full command of the German language, or if we were back in the US and they were an American family, I might feel inclined to bring up the elephant sitting around the table with us. *So, what a shock this must have been! Surprise! I sure hope we all get to know each other and hang out like a real family. What d'ya think?*

For the weeks leading up to this meeting, I've spent days hiking and biking through the vast acres of vineyards by Michael's house, obsessing if Father's family will accept me. It's what I do well, obsessing. Like a pinwheel spinning in the wind of feverish thought. Hope, fear, and failure created images that morphed into whatever state of mind was prevalent on any given day. Evenings found me exhausted from the possibilities.

Hours and hours were spent journaling or staring off into nothingness while I tried to pull up those memories about my father that seem to be gone forever. Discovering him was not part of the story when this journey began. My focus had been on Sieglinde's long-kept secret, the story that my cousins and I felt needed to be thoroughly examined and accepted. Now my aunt and I have stories that entwined. Lifetimes of introspection to wade through. Sieglinde's search for her father ended very differently; her closure took place in a graveyard. I have chances here. Today is only the beginning. I hope and pray my father's family can find it in their hearts to accept me.

Father sits at the head of the table and leads the conversation. He talks about this town he loves and has lived in since his retirement from the *Bundesdruckerei,* the state-owned printing department of official documents. A famous resort town in Western Germany, Bad Nauheim is known as a destination for health and rejuvenation. It's where Elvis lived when he served in the Army. The town was also a residential area for American occupation forces after World War II. It was totally spared from Allied bombing despite its proximity to Frankfurt and Hitler's command complex. Rumor has it that President Roosevelt loved the town so much from his visits here before the war, that he ordered it spared. But mostly, Father says with a chuckle, "it's a great place for old folks to live."

As Father addresses my cousin, I turn to my half-brother and ask if he speaks English. He shakes his head and opens his hands on the table. I turn to his son Niklas—English is mandatory in German schools—and ask him.

He blushes and shakes his head. "No, English is not easy for me, sorry."

I glance at Bettina who smiles hugely and shakes her head, and finally Anni, who purses her lips and also gives a quick shake. I tell them I speak German, only badly—*ha ha*—and get quick nods before they turn away again. I can't seem to hold eye contact long enough to make the connection I desperately want. Or perhaps my German is a garbled mess. What I do know are simple everyday phrases and words. I resolve to change this. But now I think their reticence is protective in nature. I'm an intrusion.

Father orders an Austrian specialty—a concoction called a Kaiserschmarrn which is a cross between pancakes and waffles: doughy layers with raisins and a side of vanilla cream to pour on top. The others order the daily special—wiener schnitzel. I order a salad that I hope I can choke down. Father chatters happily, occasionally throwing a few American phrases my way. It sounds like he's juggling marbles in his mouth. He tells me his English is limited to what American soldiers taught him, so he can't repeat much of it, *heh, heh.* I will soon find out that he was a POW captured on the beaches of Normandy in 1944. His English was learned out of necessity.

At breaks in the conversation I glance around but no one seems inclined to chime in, although occasional soft comments I can't understand are directed at each other. Everyone looks pleasant enough, but there's no doubt this is my father's party. He's having the time of his life.

Still, I'm relieved when the meal is over and he suggests a walk through the surrounding park. He takes off through the open glass doors and promptly trips on the base of a movable light fixture set up on the veranda. My cousin is next to him and grabs his arm. Anni shakes her head. The rest of the family act like nothing happened. I guess they're used to his miscalculations. Father has age-related macular degeneration. He's able to see peripherally, but direct vision gives him at best a blurry outline. Glasses help some. But I'll soon learn that he confidently walks familiar streets, even alone through the parks, or to the library, or his favorite Backerei where he sips coffee and chats with anyone within range.

My trim and confident father strides briskly across the veranda and down the path into the adjoining rose garden. Strolling is out of the question. I'm glad I have comfortable shoes on. Bettina walks heavily, rolling from her right hip on a leg that's at an awkward angle, a problem with her hip. Dressed in a dark-blue long-sleeved blouse and black slacks, her pleasant face becomes bright red as beads of sweat trace a path to her chin. Periodically, Father stops and whips around to make sure we're all still there. Then he's off again, his family V'd out behind him like a flock in flight. Niklas carries a small video camera Walter handed to him when we set off. He hangs back dutifully every few minutes to catch what he can while Father talks and points.

We get to a park that contains a white rectangular concrete basin filled with water that my father explains is a Kneipp pool. With a short wall in the middle and railings on either side, it is designed for walking through. We watch as a young woman gathers up her skirts, exposing long white legs, and marches slowly through. The pool and medicinal flower garden surrounding it are attributed to an early pioneer of holistic health, Sebastian Kneipp. A Bavarian priest from the nineteenth century, Father Kneipp is considered a forefather of the naturopathic medicine movement. Understanding connections between body, mind, and spirit, he developed programs incorporating whole food, exercise, and a calm mind. He also developed a hydrotherapy program named after him. My father is a frequent visitor to the pools. Now he demonstrates.

"You have to make like a stork." He rolls up his pant legs and descends three steps into the pool. Water reaches his knees. He lifts his right leg high and mindfully steps forward in a rolling motion. Repeats with left. "Come on," he yells over his shoulder. A huge grin splits his face and I think of a young boy enjoying the small pleasures in life.

I grin back and shake my head, *not today*, *Papa*. Love that he's so delighted. Wonder if he is always this way, or is he simply happy that I'm there? I hope I'll have the chance to find out. My cousin is the only taker. Eight steps on four snow-white legs take them down, around and back out. I stick a finger in; the water is ice cold. I lean against the timber edge of a raised herb garden and click away with my phone camera.

A few side glances through overlarge sunglasses: Niklas resembles his mother, with a handsome round face and a stout stature; my half-brother resembles our father—what he probably looked like as a younger man. His wavy brown hair has tiny touches of gray, short on top and the sides, longer at the back and coming down his neck to curl back up, reminding me of a cute pig's tail. He sports an impressive mustache. Anni is petite with white hair cut short and soft around her face. She stares off thoughtfully, perhaps wishing the day was over. Perhaps wishing it never had to happen at all. I caught that same look several times in the restaurant. I sense a patience born out of my father's patriarchal rule. The meeting more a duty than a choice.

Once again, I note that everyone keeps a poker face. Politeness for a stranger. Which, of course, I am. But I'm churning to ask questions, to find out what this new family does, what they love, what we may have in common. I know I will discover all these things about Papa; his openness and enjoyment of sharing his interests bubble over this afternoon. His desire to share himself with me is obvious. His regret at turning me away initially has turned into a happy second chance. I stick close and enjoy him.

After a couple of walk-throughs in the pool, we take off to visit a Graduation Tower, also called a Thorn House: a tall and long rectangular structure composed of bundles of blackthorn brushwood encased within it. Saltwater trickles down the sides and partly evaporates, leaving a white residue of mineral salts. Visitors can walk or sit in chairs in front of the tower to breathe in droplets for their touted therapeutic effects. A sign states *welcome to the rejuvenating seaside air.* Papa takes us around the structure to a water wheel which keeps briny spring water flowing. He gesticulates and explains a complicated process to my cousin. The others wander off and gather on a bench under a large linden tree. From a distance they look wilted. I wonder what they are saying.

"So," my father suddenly claps his hands together. "Let's go have some coffee. Where are the others?" He looks around, surprised not to see them. I point to the far-off linden tree, and he nods. "*Ach ja*, it's warm today."

We return the way we came, to the same restaurant. This time, we sit outside under the large umbrellas on the terrace. A harpist is playing. I hold my breath as we wend our way to an empty table. Michael sticks close and guides my father past the light fixtures. Gratefully, we sit and order drinks. Bettina and Anni order a cooler made with seltzer, cucumber, and a sprig of basil. I compliment their choice and Bettina perks up. *What a trooper*, I think. *We've been touring now for several hours and not a peep of complaint.* Her smile never wavers. She asks for my email address. *Bless you*, I think as I write it out for her. *Thank you for a show of acceptance.*

I'm at one end of the table, next to my half-brother. "So," I say in German. "What do you do for a living?" Big smile. I'm interested and hope I'll be able to understand everything he's about to tell me.

He hesitates for a few beats, then "I work for First Data merchant services, they are based out of Atlanta. I'm a business analyst in the Frankfurt office."

In English. My mouth falls open. I hear my cousin's coffee spoon clatter onto the table. *Well, son of a bitch,* I think. I close my mouth, face flushed and confused. My brain is sparking with humiliation and anger. Did he pretend not to understand English to keep his distance? Was he eavesdropping throughout the afternoon to see what my intentions were? Or did he feel uncomfortable and wanted to wait to come forward? I imagine I'll find out in time, but for now it's best to let it go. This is not the time for a confrontation.

All I can manage is "Oh." And nod.

Later we gather back at the flat, in the living room. Father continues to lead the conversation, as the rest of my new family looks pleasantly but silently on. The scene with my brother over coffee has soured my mood. Suddenly I feel it's time to go. Guilt washes back into me at disrupting a family's anchored life. No amount of charm can work in a day's time to wash away the shock of this kind of intrusion, and I've never been accused of having abundant charm. I think it may be best to give everyone the chance to absorb the time we spent together today and see how we feel about each other. Will my brother eventually accept me? I hope so. Right now, I don't feel warm and fuzzy toward him. In fact, I can barely look at him. But I also can't blame him. What a shock this must have been.

I wonder how Anni feels and try to put myself in her place. Papa was dating her before my mother came back to Germany from Turkey with my soon-to-be stepfather. She was surely exposed to his anger and bitterness at losing his daughter and her mother to an American soldier. I wish I could tell her that fate handed him the right choice. I know she gave him happiness that Mom could not. She's someone I would like to spend time with and get to know, but I'm also aware I will always be a reminder of a beautiful woman who gave him a child. Or perhaps she simply wishes this upheaval to a settled life had never happened.

Why now, she seems to want to ask me. After a lifetime of keeping this from their only son, why now do I show up to shake up a family's life? I get a sense of quiet, pragmatic patience with her husband who is clearly pleased that his daughter rang his doorbell. Again, frustration in not being more fluent in German washes over me, the ability of clear communication is not in my grasp right now. But I determine that it will be. At some point, I hope that we can speak openly and find resolution to the feelings everyone is dealing with right now.

As we stand for goodbyes, Papa takes my hands in both of his and looks searchingly into my eyes as he asks, "Bist du enttäuscht?"

I smile hesitantly and look at Michael for interpretation because I don't know this word: *enttäuscht*.

Michael quickly answers for me, but I don't understand what he says. My father nods and we all walk down to Michael's car. Everyone waves as we drive off. We turn onto the main street and I look back. They are standing in a tight group, still waving. Smiling.

I melt into the seat, finally able to drop stiff shoulders. Rub my neck and forehead. Suddenly I realize that I have a wicked headache. "Whew! That was tough."

I ask Michael to interpret my father's last question.

"He asked if you were disappointed," he tells me slowly.

"I … I don't understand." My heart speeds up. "Why would he say that? Was my face giving me away? I did feel like no one except my father wanted to be there. It may be the language difference. But I could have muddled through if I had felt an opening in any of them. Yeah, I did get frustrated, especially when my brother and I could have talked more, since he knows English well enough. I was in shock after that little scene over coffee. I guess it hit home that I'm an unwelcome intruder here."

Michael shrugs. "It could have been worse. But I understand how you feel. Six hours together and Walter did most of the talking. You're right, the family has been shaken up. I think he's spent the last two weeks trying to share this big secret and giving everyone time to get used to it."

We sit in silence for a few minutes. I look out over the growing wheat fields as we head out of town. Everything is pristine. As we speed away, I wonder if I'll be invited back.

"I was able to pull Niklas aside," Michael continues. "I asked if they were surprised to find out about you. He said they were very shocked, especially his father, your new half-brother. They also found out Anni knew about you and never said anything."

That would explain her looks of sadness. Was it regret or feelings of being caught in the middle? Perhaps my father had demanded, of himself and of her, that this accidental child be forgotten, along with the vitriol my crazed and angry mother had hurled at him when she discovered herself pregnant. Why in the world *would* he have told his son about me? He never expected to see me again.

"I told him it was a long day for you. That you had been too excited to sleep well last night, so maybe we can get together again soon." Michael looks over at me and grins. "More family secrets. You know, like ours; what we are finding out now about our grandfather after all these years. For Walter's family it's almost worse because now you will be a part of their lives, and they don't know yet what you're all about. They were watching and deciding today. The key will be what happens next. Give it time," he tells me wisely.

Michael accelerates onto the autobahn, and we speed towards the comfort of my cousin's home. Ivonne is waiting with homemade vegetable soup and a chilled bottle of white wine. We'll sit around and chat about the day, the joys and the challenges. Thoughts turn to the woman who flirted with the camera. The dark-haired girl who charmed my father with her thirst for adventure and a toss of her hair. It seemed impossible to reconcile this afternoon's images with the mother I had known.

Disparate Profiles

Journal
2016

She grew up with dreams, my mother did, of a life that did not include a child and husband. Instead of a home and family, she saw four walls closing in. Instead of love and support, she saw only relegation. Susi worked hard to evade marriage. I wonder now if it was because of her mother's participation in creating children for the Third Reich. Or perhaps it was because, as the oldest, she had too many responsibilities at too young an age. More than love and commitment, she desired freedom.

There was a young man who came to her family's home when she was only sixteen and begged her to marry him. When she refused, he left their flat. A few minutes later, she and her mother heard a loud thump in the attic. Running up to investigate, they found him in a heap on the floor—with a broken arm—after he fell from the rafters where he tried to hang himself with a tie that tore.

There was a Sheik's son in Baghdad who plied her with jewelry and repeatedly asked her to become his wife. She considered this one because, she said, he was very rich and handsome. But no, her life would have been unbearably constricted; just one of his wives, part of a harem. These and other stories were told to me by my half-sister Jackie. They were close, Mom and Jackie, so it wasn't surprising that Jackie recently had another story for me, one I had not heard about before, that my mother had shared with her years ago.

I will try to reconstruct the words as Mom's voice comes to me:

I took my shoes off. It was late afternoon and I needed something from the store—I don't remember what it was. I reached a park and decided to take off my sandals to feel the grass between my toes. I didn't notice him until he had me in a choke hold. He dragged me into the bushes and held his arm on my throat so I couldn't scream. I knew I would die. After he was done, he flipped me onto my stomach and wrapped a chain tightly around my neck, cutting into my throat. I passed out. I guess he thought I was dead. It was starting to get dark when I woke up and made my way back to the hotel we were staying at. My roommate was getting dressed for the evening performance when I stumbled in. She took me to the hospital.

She was not allowed to file charges. She was told it was her fault; a young woman shouldn't walk the streets alone in Ankara, Turkey. Not even in daytime. Not even to go to the store.

This wasn't the first time she was raped. At the age of fourteen, Susi cleaned rooms at a small inn located in the next town over to help with expenses at home. She befriended a girl who invited her over one afternoon after work. When she arrived, the girl's brother ambushed and assaulted her while the friend helped hold her down. The brother and sister were the mayor's children. My mother was told her life, and her family's life, would be ruined if she reported the attack. The year was 1946, and post-war life was difficult enough. She kept quiet.

The second rape was almost more than she could bear, and her new world became as painful as her old. In Turkey there were no more nighttime heart-pounding races to the bunker listening to the bombs as they whistled down, trying to figure out how close they would land. No more standing in line for food rations, hoping there would be something left besides rotten onions (Oh, why didn't she get there sooner!). No more cleaning and washing all day for garrisoned SS Officers and then coming home to do it all over again. But the pain was there in other ways, and she was tired.

The timing was perfect for Ted McKrill, who had gone to the supper club in Ankara where my mother's dance troupe was performing. He instantly fell in love with the tiny brunette with the big smile. He said they met before, in a club in Beirut, but she didn't recall. He swore that he couldn't forget. Twenty-four hours later he proposed. And proposed again. The third time, Susi said yes.

•

When I was young and people commented that I looked like my mother, fear would grip my heart. I saw an unwanted future in her gaunt cheeks, in the furrows between the faded blue of anxious eyes, in the pointed nose prominent above a delicate mouth now offset by vertical smoker lines. In my teens, when Mom was not yet forty, sadness had replaced the luster of youth with the brittle stubbornness of one who feels cheated by life, but insists on battling it daily. My mother knew how to wring every last drop out of her emotions. I was ashamed of her. Her struggle with the English language made her sound uneducated and lowly. She seemed harsh; loving gentleness did not seem possible.

By the time I was ready to start third grade, we relocated to an armed forces base in Sagamihara, on the island of Honshu in Japan. By now I spoke English fluently, read voraciously, had won a spelling bee, and began writing stories. I had a friend or two, was the neighborhood tetherball menace (still tall and skinny) and hung out with a new Dachshund puppy named Bitsy. I had a new baby brother named Patrick, named in honor of my stepfather's Irish heritage. He was adorable and I doted on him, this brother I'd always wanted. He demanded his mother's constant attention. Once he got it, his face would split into a satisfied grin.

Mom soon became pregnant again with a little girl she named Jacqueline, and we called Jackie. It was about this time that she quit wearing makeup. Clothes were thrown on haphazardly. Except when Ted took her to the Officer's Club for dinner. Then she wore fashionable dresses that attracted attention to her tiny waist and long legs. Black eye-liner enhanced her pale blue eyes, soft-colored lipstick her thin lips. She turned heads. And hardened hearts. The other wives resented her, some out of jealousy perhaps. Some because she was German. Me too. I wanted her to be American. That's all.

I was ashamed of being German. The first time I saw footage of Hitler, I was shocked for days. How could someone who looked like a raving caricature possibly rule a country, *my* country? I thought about my quiet life with Oma in a little town with folks who also seemed to live quietly, and was baffled. There was the ache of looking in the mirror and seeing a German child, one whose looks might never match the American ideal. A transformative discovery imprinted a dissatisfaction with my features that I still suffer from today.

In 1963, during our first tour in Japan, I was eight years old and home alone. I can't remember the circumstances; where my mother and new baby brother were. My step-father must have been at work. I began going through cabinets I previously had no interest in. Not sure what I was searching for; probably something to pass the time, but also to ground me, to help me understand this new world I was living in which was so different from what I had known. I found the usual knick-knacks, odds and ends. And my stepfather's Playboys. A large stack.

Not knowing what they were, I grabbed one off the top, randomly flipped it open. And there she was: the broad face with a petite upturned nose, full red lips in a big smile. She was shown from the waist up, big brown eyes gazing warmly into the camera. A red and white gingham checked blouse covered her arms but draped off her shoulders like a shawl. The blouse was unbuttoned; her full bosom spilled out like it had no choice in the matter.

Who was she? Why was she posing like this? Thoughts ran wild. Nerves prickled. I looked down at my oh-so-skinny self, suddenly painfully aware of my pale blue eyes, deep-set and small. A prominent nose that flared large at the tip. Thin lips. All of which were framed in a small oval face topped by mousy brown hair. *I will never be an American girl.*

All blame went to my mother.

•

In 1965, the summer I turned ten, the Army relocated us to paradise. It was the time of British rock bands, Dick Clark's Where the Action Is, Radio KPOI and Wolfman Jack, the Young Rascals, The Beach Boys, and the height of the Vietnam War. Our family moved into a small clapboard house high on a hill overlooking Honolulu. Ted was officially stationed at Schofield Barracks on the island of Oahu, but for most of the two years we lived there, he was hunkered down somewhere at the southern border of North Vietnam, listening to and interpreting enemy chatter. He was gone for close to a year, then returned home for a month.

One night, I woke to whispering in the kitchen. I could tell it was Ted, but he didn't sound at all like the strong, commanding man I was used to. His strident whispers seemed to go on forever, until they finally stopped. Sobbing began. I slipped out of bed and crept to the kitchen door. There was my tiny mother sitting in his massive lap, hugging him tightly and consoling him with soft shushing noises, as if he were a child.

Soon he left again for another tour.

Mom struggled with the responsibilities that were now hers alone. Groceries had to be bought, bills had to be paid, and the children had doctor's appointments. The house was barely finished. The red clay yard needed to be planted with grass and hibiscus. Jackie was turning a year old, and Patrick was an overactive toddler. My mother had only recently learned to drive.

Stress unfolded in waves, although I was too immersed in my own problems to notice.

I attended school at August Ahrens Elementary in a small town called Waipahu. It lay at the bottom of the hill from our neighborhood, and you could count on one hand the number of non-native children in each of my classes. We were labeled *haoles* and reaction to us ranged from dislike to contempt. For the first time I realized my German-ness was irrelevant; the disdain doled out to me was equal to other non-native classmates. We learned about Hawaii's history in school. I also muddled my way through Michener's epic history tome, *Hawaii,* in an attempt to understand where hatred for white skin came from. I knew that many Hawaiians resented being a part of the United States. All my ten-year-old brain could come up with was the difference in culture. Years later I decided that, as with all things different and forced upon someone, the root of hatred is fear of loss of culture, of contrast in beliefs and customs, of losing a familiar way of life. In other words, a loss of identity. This I understood.

Classmates (and their parents) frequently commented about how fair I was. It was not a compliment. With two small children in tow, it was a hardship for Mom to provide daily rides to school and back home. I often rode with a neighborhood girl. After school one afternoon, as I was heading to her mother's car, a native boy grabbed my book bag, chanting *Haole go home.* A group formed around us. No one intervened. Not a parent, not a teacher. His chasing and taunting seemed to go on forever. I burst into tears as the book bag was thrown at my feet amidst titters of laughter. On the drive home, I sat head down, nauseous and ashamed of my white knobby knees, white arms and hands tucked between them.

At home, Mom was mired in her own world, spinning in one place, and waiting for her husband to come home alive. Then suddenly, she seemed to mellow out, gain a bit of weight (Mom always hovered around ninety to a hundred pounds), and settle into the paradise around us. Years later, I found out she had been put on the anti-depressant Elavil, which explained the sudden change in her demeanor. Occasionally we drove to a nearby shoreline, a private cove where Jackie and Patrick splashed in the turquoise water. I watched them while Mom stared peacefully, but vacantly, into the horizon.

My beloved Oma flew from Germany to help out. I had not seen her since I was seven. Now she seemed a stranger as I tried to impress her with my new American ways. I could no longer speak fluent German; she knew no English. I felt a deep distance between us. The lost German child was now out to prove herself a self-sufficient American girl. Shortly after her arrival, Oma and I sat on the lanai and watched Patrick and Jackie as they dug into their box of toys. Mom was out running errands. Suppertime came and went. I announced that I was in charge of supper tonight and dug through the pantry until I found a can of soup. I dumped it into a pot, placed it on the stove, and turned up the heat. And promptly forgot about it. When my mother arrived home, she found a blackened mess on the stove. We were all still on the lanai, oblivious to the smoke and smell.

During Oma's stay, adolescent hormones kicked in and gave me attitude. I no longer reached out for her arms to hug me, more concerned with clothes and the latest pop songs on the radio than wanting to spend much time with her. I was unhappy with my home life and thought often of running away. Instead of turning to her for comfort, I was following my mother's path of insisting on independence and freedom. Love and commitment were not part of the equation.

Ted returned home from Vietnam in the summer of 1967. We packed up our belongings, sold the house and prepared for Ted's relocation to Vint Hill Farms in Virginia. This would be my first time on the mainland. The war overseas continued. Mom remained in turmoil, and Oma came with us to help take care of the children. We flew into San Francisco. Ted bought a Vista Cruiser station wagon and a pop-up camper, and we drove to Virginia. What a wonder this country was to me: Los Angeles, San Bernadino, New Mexico, Las Vegas, Nevada, Arizona; then Texas, Louisiana, Mississippi, Alabama, Florida, South Carolina and finally Virginia. We saw the redwoods, lush forests, the Grand Canyon, desert, miles of corn and farmland, open spaces the like of which I had never seen.

During this time, Oma was busy with Patrick and Jackie. Mom seemed to sleep quite a bit, (she was still on Elavil) and Ted fiddled with the camper and the car, checking maps for our next stop. I wandered through nature by myself and met other kids on the campgrounds. Oma and I slept in the back of the station wagon. I listened to pop music on a portable radio and rambled on about the Monkees, the Young Rascals, and other favorite groups. Sleep always came quickly, and I sensed that Oma was always tired.

She flew back to Germany when we reached Virginia. Three years later she died alone at her home in Montabaur from congestive heart failure. When Mom told me the news of her death, I sat in my room, thinking about our time together. Of how much love I had felt when I was in her care. And what an ass I had been when she stayed with us. I could have turned to her for the love I felt I was missing and that, perhaps, she needed as well.

The winter that year in Virginia was one of the coldest in history and much of our time was spent waiting out blizzards. The darkness and cold added to Mom's misery.

•

One year later we relocated back to Japan, this time on the southern island of Kyushu. This tour was the longest yet, two and half years. One fine sunny day, right after my fifteenth birthday, I came home from school to hysterical laughter as I approached the front door to our small clapboard house. And thuds. More laughter. My mother's usually immaculate living room was a jumble of couch cushions, pillows, and toys. Patrick and Jackie were running through the rooms screeching in hysterical excitement at being unsupervised. Puzzled, I headed to the kitchen, only to find it empty. I called and searched until I found my parents' bedroom door locked. No answer when I yelled Mom over and over. I managed to dial the numbers to Ted's office.

Later, leaning against the shattered bedroom doorframe, I stared at my mother's ashen face and slack lips as Ted held her. An empty pill bottle stood on the nightstand.

The base chaplain stopped by with his wife a few days later. It had rained. I stared at their muddy footprints as they marched across my mother's clean carpet into our parlor. I thought about how angry she would be when she got home. How she would yell at me for not asking them to take off their shoes. The chaplain and his wife sat on the divan and looked at the three of us in dismay, a fifteen year old and two small children, Ted at work. They told me how sorry they were. They told me they prayed for us and for Mom. I didn't know what to say, so I said *thank you* many times before they finally left. I thought that their prayers wouldn't help; my mother did not believe in God. I wondered where she had thought she was going.

Mom came home. I wish I could say I stayed by her side, helping her with the household chores, offering comfort to Patrick and Jackie. They were quiet now, eyes large in small faces. Instead I ran from the sadness in our home, gone until late at night, hanging out at the Youth Center and with friends. Home suffocated me in fear.

Once again, my mother had tried to leave me.

Susi in the middle, the dance troupe performing at a supper club at an undisclosed location in the Middle East, circa 1958.

Homecoming

Montabaur
July 2016

I'm staying with Cousin Michael and his wife Ivonne in their lovely town of narrow cobblestone streets and acres upon acres of vineyards. Located about an hour and half from Bad Nauheim and my father's flat, Michael's large home is the perfect base when I come to Germany. It is a place of laughter, music, and wine. Ivonne cooks delicious meals and listens to our adventures, offers opinions, and keeps us grounded while her husband plays chauffeur, interpreter, and analyst.

Today we are in his car, bumping along the old streets through town as we head towards the autobahn. Our windows are down, and the early morning cool air is refreshing. The weather has been unusually warm, and we have kept the fans going. There is no air conditioning. Michael cranks up the radio and sings along with some eighties ditty on the radio. I roll my eyes as he does a few whoop-whoop circles with his arms before regaining control of the VW Polo's steering wheel. I laugh and am reminded how much I enjoy his company.

Michael and I have known each other since he came with his family to visit Disney World in 1977, when he was an inquisitive and bright-eyed twelve-year-old to my already married and world-weary twenty-two. I'm drawn to his brash sense of humor and his generous spirit.

Currently, Ivonne is a caretaker for her father who has Alzheimer's. He lives with them in his own suite of rooms. A large picture window offers a gorgeous view of the nearby mountains which he believes are the mountains of his Chilean childhood. Ivonne rarely leaves his side; she knows his time is limited. Ivonne has an inherent nurturing soul, offset by her wild curly black hair and confident air. She offers her full support as Michael and I envelop ourselves in this quest for family discovery.

Today we are on our way to visit our uncle Hans Herbert, Oma Katharina's youngest. He and his wife Irma live close to Montabaur, the town where Oma raised her children. Michael's mother, Christel, is meeting us there. We'll drive to Oma's old quadplex. I plan to ring the doorbell and impose on the folks living there now and, hopefully, walk through the rooms my child's eyes remember. Perhaps new memories will come forward. It's possible some of my old ones won't hold up, but it's a chance I must take.

We park in front of my uncle's three-story walk-up, newly painted a charcoal color. White shutters offer a crisp contrast. The apartment building is overshadowed by the remains of a huge old warehouse and fronted by unused railroad tracks. It has rained recently. Now that the sun is out and beating down on the massive rafters of the warehouse, the heavy smell of old wood permeates the air. As we pull up, Christel hangs out of a window and yoo-hoos. We wave before making our way up the rain-slicked steps.

Irma and Christel rush forward with hugs while Hans Herbert, or Hans as we all call him, stands back in a corner of the neatly furnished parlor, observing shyly. Then he comes forward to give me a bear hug. There he is, with that crooked grin, those mischievous eyes. What on earth does a seventy-year-old man have to be mischievous about? An image pops into my mind of the brash boy I had such a crush on in my earliest memories. He is still here, although his lanky good looks have filled out from too much beer and rich food. Hans spent his life as a master baker and chef. We hug, grin at each other, and settle in on the sectional while Irma places bowls of fruit and glasses of sparkling water on the coffee table.

I talk about our plan to visit our old home, how well I remember it and hope it's still the same. He nods. "Not much you can do with a rectangular stucco building except paint it. It's probably still yellow, as it always was. Never fancy, always solid."

I hope he's right. It's comforting to my inner child that the only place I remember as dependable still is.

Hans remembers the day my mother dropped me off. The yelling, the tears, the angry whispers. Then, a small bundle in Katharina's arms. Mom relied on her mother as she went to different cities to find work. A series of work permits necessary at the time placed her in different cities working as a waitress, or a maid in a hotel. It was in one such place that she met the woman who owned a dance troupe and decided to leave the country to find her destiny. She would go on to travel to Greece, Saudi Arabia, Egypt, Lebanon and Turkey.

"Your Oma stood on the front doorstep, raised her eyes to the heavens, and asked God why he was giving her another child to raise. Then she stared into your little face and smiled through her tears." He nods, eyes far away.

"You were a sunshine in her life, whether she wanted you or not!" he laughs, and shakes his head.

He tells me that my mother came back two years later, but he didn't know her reasons. I silently hope that maybe she wanted to build a life here, with her daughter, maybe even attempt to reconcile with my father. She worked, but it was back to menial labor and she probably felt she had regressed. Six months later she signed up for two more years with the same dance troupe, headed to Iraq and finally Ankara, where she met my stepfather.

"I never knew that she had returned after a few years away. I have no memories of it and no one has mentioned it before," I say slowly.

I venture a guess that she found the same options available upon her return: work in an inn or restaurant; marriage and household drudgery; the stigma of an unmarried mother. I see her sitting in the old kitchen, looking around at the fading wallpaper and warped linoleum floor. Remembering things that happened here along with the things that can never happen here. She may have decided then that she needed to find a husband, but one who could take her away from the life she did not want.

Ted Lewis McKrill was born Anderson, a name he gave up because he did not want to be tied to a father who didn't want him. He took his mother's maiden name, the woman who died shortly after he was born. As a child, Ted became a ward of the state of Washington, although he was fortunate enough to live with his maternal grandmother. At sixteen, he quit school and joined the circus as a laborer. At seventeen he joined the Army. Here his quiet intelligence found a home. He accelerated through the ranks to become a chief warrant officer assigned to discovering secrets, assisting the American Security Agency (which later became the National Security Agency, or NSA) during the cold war with communism. When he met my mother in the Middle East where he was stationed, destiny was there banging a big brass gong, rendering him senseless. He fell hopelessly in love and remained so for the rest of his life. He never wavered in his devotion to her.

Christel chimes in.

"Have you heard the story about the zoo?" she asks me.

I shake my head.

"Well, Ted had to pay a lot of money to buy out her contract with the dance outfit. He also gave her money to get home. He had been transferred to Frankfurt, had to leave Turkey immediately and she was to follow him. Well, she didn't show up on their agreed upon date."

Christel sighs and bites into a juicy apricot; takes a minute to wipe her chin.

Although Ted's devotion was well-known, I had always pictured Mom as responding grudgingly to his affections. Now I'll hear how she tried to ditch him. I sit back and cross my legs.

"When he finally was able to get ahold of someone back in Ankara, he was told she had left days ago. He assumed she took off. He said later he never expected to see her again. Turns out Susi ran into problems getting out of the country. She missed her plane and had trouble booking another flight. She actually got home in a roundabout way, I think. Trains, as in the Orient Express, I heard."

Christel frowns for a moment, taps her forehead as if it will help her remember.

"Anyway, she shows up around a week late and goes to the Army Post to find Ted. They won't let her enter and she pleads her story to the Military Police at the front gate. They feel sorry for her and call the barracks. Some guy there says Ted is spending his day off at the Frankfurt Zoo. Susi gets a cab and tears down to the zoo. Runs around looking for him. And finds him! She says it was just like a movie. She ran up to him and they had a tearful reunion right there in front of everyone."

She pops the remainder of the apricot into her mouth and looks around at us, quite delighted with her story. I am too. I uncross my legs and lean forward. I smile happily at Christel for sharing this. Once again, I see the person I never imagined my mother could be. Always careful with her happiness, careful of any overt display of love, careful of exposing her inner self to a world that she felt judged her harshly, Mom had dropped her pride and opened her heart.

Hans chimes in with a story of his own, although it's a far cry from romance. He remembers sitting in the parlor at their home on Kantstrasse one evening before the wedding. He was fifteen and home from his apprenticeship in a nearby town. Hans was watching television with Ted while Susi and Katharina were in and out of the room, chattering away. Under the couch was a six-pack of beer. Whenever the women weren't paying attention, Ted reached under the couch to grab an open bottle and take a long pull before putting it back. When he saw Hans watching him, he put a finger to his lips. Soon the six pack was empty, and he excused himself to veer off to bed. My mother watched him with a puzzled look, eyes narrowing as she watched him stumble off. Hans chuckles at the story. But this now sounds more like the mother I knew. I'm sure she rousted him out of a sound sleep to chastise him, the beer smell giving him away.

I'm also sure she found the empty six-pack carton, probably with Hans' help.

I don't remember excessive beer drinking in our home. True, Ted loved his beer and there was always some stashed in the back of the refrigerator. But when he reached in for one after work most evenings, he got a sharp look and comment from Mom along the lines of *Watch it buster, do you really need to have one?* To which he usually replied in an overly jovial voice, "Oh Susie Q, just one to make the food taste better," which usually prompted a comment from Mom about how she slaved away at the stove all afternoon, which should be enough to make the food taste good. The scenario seemed half in jest but there was no mistaking the underlying meaning. Mom imposed rules and restrictions, and he gave in to her as he did with most everything. In their relationship she was the boss.

•

The afternoon is moving on, and we want to get going to Oma's old home. Hans and Irma are not coming along, so there are hugs and well wishes all around. Michael and I climb back in the Polo and pull out. Christel follows us in her car. As we drive through town, I already get a sense of homecoming. Old timber-frame buildings known as *Fachwerkhäuser* are still hodge-podge along the cobble-stone streets, although modern stores on the ground floors contrast with the apartments above. Neat window boxes overflow with geraniums. I *know* this place. Oma didn't have a car. We walked everywhere. My child's eye replaces the modern shops with the old and everything is the same. Fortunately, the bombers flew over this town, leaving it intact on their way to more strategic targets like Frankfurt.

With a history that can be traced back to the year 959, a portion of the pockmarked city wall still stands. The Montabaur Castle sits high on a hill in the town center, its bright yellow walls a beacon for miles around. An archbishop-elect, returning from the Crusades in 1217, had the castle built and named it Mons Tabor for its striking likeness to Mount Tabor in Israel. Today it is a hotel and conference center. The village was granted town rights in 1291, with its own coat of arms. Now it serves as the district seat of the *Westerwaldkreis* region of Rhineland-Palatinate, and as the administrative center of a municipality that includes twenty-four communities. The once-sleepy town has a high-speed rail station, a huge outlet mall, and the AFC Fighting Farmers American football team.

We park the car at the outlet mall and walk. Christel takes the lead. At seventy-four she still has a strong stride, her wavy blond hair now cut short and sporting a reddish tint that sparks in the sunshine. After divorcing Michael's father years ago, she married a kind and grateful gentleman in his eighties. They are content together. Laughter still comes easily to her. She insists that happiness is found in the little things in life. And the right perspective.

Along the city wall to the end, we cut through a stretch of deep green woods. Past the elementary school that has been there forever. In the final years of the war it was used as a hospital but reopened as a school when the dust settled. Christel tells me that I accompanied Oma when she walked Hans here in the morning, running and hopping to keep up. Our path from home traversed long sets of steps built onto the incline of the forest, leading from the Montabaur River to the front of the school building.

This is the way we go down. I stop halfway; know I have been here. The river below us is frothing from recent rains, raging over boulders. It is bordered by a railing that wasn't there when I was a child. In winter I would push a sled downhill from our front lawn, past the garden, over Karl-Siebert-Strasse and onto the river's frozen surface. Once I fell through thin ice and was lucky enough to be pulled out by older kids who were ice skating. The terror and cold memories assail me. I feel the frigid water pull me under as I struggle to stay beneath the ice hole, grabbing and grabbing at its edges as they break. Here is where memory stops. The next image is of Oma hovering over me as I lay under a cloud of white down bedding.

I wonder how I was allowed so much freedom at four and five years old, scooting around on my sled in winter and traipsing through woods and over meadows in the summer.

•

Christel marches with purpose. Michael and I scramble to keep up. She startles us when she suddenly begins to talk about her biological father. She tosses clipped words over her shoulder, perhaps in a rush to get it all out before she changes her mind. He was a master shoemaker. He probably stayed in Katharina's attic and had a brief relationship with her outside of the essential coupling of Lebensborn. Perhaps not. Christel found out about her father when she was nineteen and needed her birth certificate to apply for her marriage license. A stranger was listed as her father on the certificate her mother gave her. Stunned, Christel confronted her mother. Katharina explained that she had been unable to collect Felix's pension after his death, so she tried to collect from Christel's biological father who had also died in the war. She may have tried to use her participation in Lebensborn to justify payments. Christel shrugs.

Both Christel and Sieglinde lived at a Deaconess Home from the age of fourteen. Sieglinde learned secretarial skills while Christel learned housekeeping (yes, it was considered a profession.) According to Christel, Sieglinde always seemed to be privileged. Sieglinde and Christel are both strong women, and I get the impression there was competition, perhaps even jealousy, between her and Christel. Sieglinde always felt, as she put it, different. As if she were an outsider. She may have had an air of superiority. Sieglinde has, and always has had, a directness and a strong sense of self-confidence, likely interpreted as condescension. I believe this may have been her self-protective coating.

My aunt declares it was a shocking discovery to find out that Felix was not her father. But she filed it away as *not worth talking about.* Since she had never known Felix, who left before she was born, one unknown father was as good as another. My head spins. I can't imagine how Michael feels, although this is by now old news. He too shrugs and says it doesn't matter so much. Later he tells me his mother never said a word before. Sieglinde's confession opened a

Pandora's Box. For Christel it is, simply and pragmatically, a fact that has been dealt with and put where it belongs: in the past.

•

Uphill and downhill we trek. My head swivels, looking for anything familiar. Up a small hill, over to Kantstrasse and suddenly we are standing in front of the building I remember so well. My heart starts to gallop. I can't breathe. An ache washes over me and settles deep in my gut. The Germans have a perfect word for what I am feeling: Heimweh, which translates into *home-ache*. More than nostalgia, Heimweh is an intense longing for the past. A strong desire, a craving to go back. Although the child I remember often felt a sense of aloneness, this place and my Oma represented love. How often I conjured up this ugly rectangular building as a castle. How often I recollected the simple rooms as a sanctuary.

The more I know about my grandmother and her enigmatic life, the more surprising the feelings of warmth and safety that wash over me as I walk around the building. There was never a sense of Oma hiding any secrets, never a sense that men came around. I glance up at the large casement window in the bedroom Oma and I shared. Warm nights snuggled in bed as we turned the pages of my beloved books. Whispers of *"Gute Nacht"* in the dark as she made her way out, leaving the door cracked so I could see the light from the kitchen as she sat and crocheted. The smell of her cigarette drifted in like perfume. Her smell.

Her mother's heart.

On the other side of the building is the kitchen window that faces the long walkway from the main street and the front of the quadplex. The window where I spent hours waiting for a father to come. This is a different kind of Heimweh, a different ache. An ache of want. An ache of need. Fractures that required a binding.

Quadplexes such as ours were built when Hitler's vision of an Aryan race was gaining a foothold in the early 1930s. Sturdy two-story buildings of wood and plaster, with flats on each end repeated up and down our hilly street. Only the colors varied, from tan to mustard to soft green to deep blue. Ours was and always had been a soft yellow, now with white shutters instead of the black I remember from my childhood.

The paint looks fresh and there is a for sale sign by the front door. For a few exhilarating minutes I toy with the idea of buying it, moving in and living the rest of my life in the past. Michael, who often and uncannily seems to be able to read my mind, raises an eyebrow and points to the sign, his grin teasing.

"Well, not practical." I finally say. "Memories are enough. My life is elsewhere, and everyone knows you can't go home again."

This last line as a quip, with a chuckle to offset the ache in my gut. The ding-dong of the doorbell rewards us with a dog barking deep inside on the first floor. But no one answers. It's likely the upstairs flat is empty while waiting for a new owner. We ring again, just to be sure. Take our time to look around. The black, loamy soil of the old vegetable garden now supports roses, dahlias, cockle bells, chamomile, and yarrow. Gone is the hedge of prickly gooseberries I took care to stay away from, letting Oma pick the tart fruit I then gobbled by the handful. Gone the rows of strawberry plants. Gone the trellis supporting the raspberry bushes.

Ten steep steps and a railing take me down to the cellar door. Two big bags of trash are heaped in front. The door is locked. Oh, how I would love to go in! The musty dirt smell is still there, I'm sure. I wonder if the ancient wooden shelves and bins are there, or if they have been replaced with new plastic ones. And the potting table, is it still there?

That potting table. An image drifts in, of the child in the room with dusty windows and a wooden table used to prepare seedlings. The child is sprawled on the table, but she is not alone. A young boy close to her age is with her. He stands in front of her but he's looking away, at the wall. His hands are busy inside her dress with the white pinafore she must wear when Oma has company. Whose idea was it to play doctor? Who was the boy? Did I get to examine him, too? I think back on a strong childhood curiosity about boys, to the point of wishing I was one so that I too could have the kind of freedom I felt they had.

Christel, in her usual practical fashion, looks unaffected by the memories that must surely be flooding her as she stands in front of her childhood home. They are there, as we know. But she has brought us here because I asked. As she looks around, I don't see any signs of nostalgia, aching or otherwise. The strength of Sieglinde and Christel astounds me. They adopted their poker faces and kept them to survive in *those times*. After the war, they found laughter and fulfillment in their families and the joys of everyday life. Were these inherited traits from their supposedly genetically superior fathers? Or simply the strengths passed on from their mother?

Susi and her two sisters, Gunda and Erika, suffered from depression and anxiety. Did they inherit these traits from Felix? Or were they traumatized by reality and hardships of war? Born in 1932, 1934, and 1936 respectively, they knew hunger, fear, and death at formative ages. What had they seen? What had they experienced? They were surely aware of their father's anguish when he left home after discovering his wife's infidelity.

Gunda and Erika both married young. Gunda moved with her family to Switzerland, and Erika moved to Cologne. Aside from knowing them as a child and meeting them again briefly in 1983, my aunts were almost strangers to me. They distanced themselves from their mother and siblings. Erika died from undisclosed health problems in 2010. The family was not informed at the time of her death; it only came to light later. Gunda has been in and out of mental health care facilities for depression since her husband died, also in 2010. No one left seems to know more of this estranged family.

On the drive back to Michael's house, I ponder the story that Christel told us about the zoo. Images run through my mind. Mom in her (probably) high heels and fancy dress running frantically around the various animal exhibitions, looking for a large man, probably in uniform even on his day off. Her desperate need to let him know she loved him and had come for him. How powerful the emotions must have been when they were finally back in each other's arms.

It's a different viewpoint I have now, in contrast to all the sadness and emptiness I saw that prompted me to leave home and marry at eighteen. I moved eight hours away, to a small Florida panhandle town where my new husband lived, and only came home as my marriage began to disintegrate. This was also the time I first met my cousin Michael and his family when they came to Orlando in 1977. I showed up while they were there. After two weeks and many theme parks later, I went back home to give my crumbling marriage one more chance. A year later we gave up and began divorce proceedings.

Soon I moved to St. Petersburg, Florida, and began college classes. Ted offered to help me with finances. I gratefully accepted. For a while, Mom called every few weeks. The conversation always began with a long moment of silence, then a sigh. "Hello, Madlen." I would answer, "Mom. How are you?" Another short silence, then, "All right … I guess." This was my cue to ask what the problem was. And she would launch into all the current aggravations that life was tossing at her. Often, they were medical. Mom seemed to suffer from many ailments that were stomach-related. Arthritis also ran the length of her body: her fingers, the base of her neck, her lower back. I don't remember her asking me what was going on in my life. Usually, she was still going through her litany when I would beg off and hang up. After a while, I anticipated her calls and did not answer the phone. Regret runs through me, but at the time I could do no different.

Conversation with a New Brother

Bad Nauheim
December 2016

We are at a charming restaurant called The Teichhaus, in a private room with twenty-five guests, celebrating my father's ninetieth birthday. Cousin Michael has accompanied me. He is still recovering from his company Christmas party the night before, eyes glazed and red-rimmed. He and I spent the afternoon yesterday wandering in and out of shops, looking for birthday gifts for my father. What do you give a man who has simple tastes and has collected trinkets from extensive travel around the world?

Michael picked up a specialty oil and vinegar set because he thought my father liked salads. (Turns out Papa limits his salad intake because he has diverticulosis, another menace of his advanced age along with his eyesight and hearing.) I settled on a handmade market basket to hold the oil and vinegar, a small addition to his main gift: a photo album I made through Shutterfly, which chronicled milestones in my life.

I had spent weeks going through old albums to pick out photos that best illustrated my life throughout the decades, beginning with the few baby pictures my mother had given me. After these, I added the only one of me as a teenager, my brown hair long and straight, parted in the middle. I'm sprawled on my bed, leaning back onto an arm, one leg crossed over the other, and encased in a pair of bell-bottoms circa 1973.

I proudly displayed my University of South Florida diploma, edges a bit ragged. I left out any photos from my first marriage, choosing instead a shot or two taken during my corporate sales career, a time of being single and driven by accomplishment. The remainder showed my happy second marriage, travels with my husband and son, and ended with one at the business we built together. A carefully chosen lifetime that any father could be proud of. Beautifully bound in a large twelve by twelve hardback book and illustrated with what I hoped were grammatically correct German captions. It loomed over his pile of gifts in a massive polka-dotted box adorned with a festive ribbon. Unable to come up with any more ideas for my new Papa, I picked up a soft scarf for Anni and a double-sided silver frame for my new brother.

This birthday bash is an all-day affair with a buffet brunch, a walk around the adjoining pond, a visit to the Weihnachtsmarkt in a nearby park, and a return for coffee and cake this afternoon. The guests had received an enthusiastic introduction to "meine Tochter aus Amerika." Some looked surprised. Others acted as if they knew already. I smiled, shook hands warmly, and looked directly into eyes that covered thoughts I could do nothing about. One older gentleman, taken aback, exclaimed *ah* loudly and looked around for my father's wife, Anni. *Was I really his daughter?* He chuckled, took my hand, and asked if Anni had known about me—*heh heh, wink wink*? To which she coolly responded from somewhere nearby, "Oh yes, I knew about her from the beginning." I smiled brightly as I slid my hand out of his.

I'm thankful and fortunate that Walter has so openly accepted me and feels no shame in explaining my existence. I feel his love reaching out for me whenever we get close. There was no hesitancy from the moment I told him who I was. And now Anni shows her support. Acceptance. Validation. Worth.

•

I returned from Munich two days ago. A train ride through lovely snow-covered country, from Michael's house to stay with Thomas for a week, then back in time for the party. While there, Thomas, his two boys, Rafi and Matteo, and I drove to Sulzbach to visit Sieglinde. We took walks through the winter landscape, returning home to defrost and warm ourselves in Sieglinde's homey kitchen with delicious food and hot tea and cocoa. Conversation led back to Katharina and the choices she made. I wanted to be certain I had understood her story

A discrepancy popped up when Sieglinde brought up Felix. At one point, she had insisted that Felix and Katharina had never divorced. Yet Christel insisted they did. That Katharina only agreed to the divorce if both Sieglinde and Christel could take the Fornoff name, even though he was not their biological father. She did not want them to be illegitimate. I wonder if she was concerned that the girls would be taken from her, to be placed in a more stable home, to be properly "Germanized."

The confusion may have occurred because Sieglinde insists that she accompanied her mother when she tried to collect Felix's pension, where they were told that he was a traitor to his country by committing suicide and was not entitled to it. Katharina always insisted that he committed suicide because of the war. Now Sieglinde concedes that maybe they had divorced. Perhaps she had misunderstood. Confirmation may have been in Katharina's paperwork, all of which Hans Herbert insists he tossed after she died. I wonder what else may have come out in those documents.

This led me to think about my own beginning, as an illegitimate child. The paperwork my brother Patrick sent to me after my stepfather died. My father had to legally agree to have no claim on me, and although he paid support (even after my mother remarried) he was not to contact me. Is it any wonder that he didn't share my existence with his only son?

As I'm pondering about this, sitting in a reverie of time lost and time found, I sense him, with a whoosh, occupy the chair our father had moments ago vacated. I look into my half-brother's eyes, so very like my own: blue-green, rather small and deep-set; his behind black square spectacles, mine behind brown.

"So," his English words tumble out. "How often do you plan to come to Germany for two to three weeks at a time?"

Bemused, I wonder what he's really asking. I tilt my head and look at him, questioning.

"I mean, you were here this past summer and now you're back. I just heard you're planning to come again next summer."

Still turning things over in my mind, I remain silent.

"I don't know about you, but I was very shocked to find out I had a sister."

He looks away and runs a hand through his dark, wavy hair with the little curly tail. I watch his hand move until the curl is patted back into place, a bit nervously. A few strands of gray give him age dignity. His eyes are wary but determined. This is the first time we have been in direct conversation, and I find myself pleased that he approached me. The thought hits me that he's been waiting for this opportunity, and he jumps right in.

"At first I told my father we needed to check on you. Here in Germany, we have had fraud, where people come around and claim they are relatives and then say they are in trouble and need money. But he said, no, no, he had a daughter with someone a long time ago and he knew it was you."

It slowly dawns on me that he had hoped one visit would be enough. Now that I had met my father I could go back to my American life. Yet here I was, five months later in December, with plans to return next July. Ah. Now I understand. They are a close-knit family. My unknown existence must have seemed unthinkable. My heart plummets as my mind scrambles. I'm a perceived threat. But why, exactly? Affection? As happy as my father seems to be that I have come back into his life, our time together can never make up for a lifetime of memories that my brother and father share, that bond I can never hope to have. Money? The fraud thing aside, I don't expect to inherit a dime. I would, someday when the time comes, love to have the album with the photos of me and my mother.

I think my brother is kind behind his doubtful eyes. Perhaps this is his way of showing me he is on the path to acceptance. To share why he was so rigid at our first meeting. His father, seemingly an honorable man, has turned out to be a man of secrets. This is probably what my brother has a problem coming to terms with. I appreciate this attempt at discourse. It's more than I've done so far.

"Michael, I've spent a lifetime wondering about my father. Now that I've finally found him, I want to get to know him. This summer I'll rent an apartment here in town for a few weeks. Then we can spend time together whenever he wants. But I can't be gone from home too long. My husband and I own a business, and I volunteer a lot at a local animal shelter walking dogs and I'm, well, busy. I've written children's books and do readings at elementary schools. For free."

I'm rambling. Sheesh. Why do I feel the need to validate myself as a nice person? A busy person who doesn't have time to try to win away the affection and whatever else he thinks I may be after? Guilt. My appearance has caused a major shitstorm in this family's life. Father is handling it well. He seems proud of me and has pushed aside the stigma of any prurient speculation. This is not happening easily for my brother. And all the friends and relatives here will need some type of explanation for my existence, if not today then on a follow-up phone call or visit.

My brother asks about my family's business. I explain that we install high-tech security systems; a lot of our work is for the government and theme parks in Orlando. He seems to like this. Perhaps I won't be asking for money after all.

"You know Michael, parents don't tell their children everything. Surely Niklas doesn't know everything about you, and I certainly haven't told my son everything about my life." I chuckle and roll my eyes. *Wink wink, heh heh.* It's also a reminder that Niklas is keeping his distance from me, avoiding eye contact. Not sure if this is because of who I am, or what I am—a new blight on the wholesome family. Perhaps he's embarrassed at my presence and thinks I should be kept hidden.

My brother looks pointedly at my silly smile.

"To buy a new car and not say anything is one thing; to have a daughter—a sister for me—is something you tell."

I wonder if it would have been more painless had I rang Father's bell thirty years ago when all of us were younger and still going through all the changes life throws at us. *Not now*, my brother seems to say. *Not when I've spent my entire life not knowing this very important fact about my father's life.* Cool blue eyes narrow as he sits and studies me. I want to turn a flushed face away, to leave the room or at least get another glass of champagne. Instead, we sit and lock eyes.

At this point our happy, oblivious father comes back. Michael attempts a smile and scoots back into his chair to the right of our father. I look down at a plate of grilled salmon, sautéed Brussel sprouts, and simmered carrots, now cold. My hunger is gone. Maybe fresh air can unclench my gut. And my recurring guilt at the upheaval I've caused in their family.

I ask Father if we can take a walk through the festivities in the adjoining park to enjoy crafts and imbibe in Glühwein, that sweet and potent Yuletide concoction of red wine and spices. Everything is already dazzling with white lights though it's barely afternoon. I look around for my cousin Michael to join us. We slip into our coats. I link one arm through Father's and the other through my cousin's. My brother rises to join us. Nerves prickle again. It takes a moment for me to realize this is a good opportunity to get to know each other better.

As my cousin and father chatter away behind us, my brother and I walk in tandem. I point out the bare beauty of this winter landscape. Sweet chestnut trees, commanding in summer, now sit as bony caricatures. The linden trees are bare of their healing leaves and frivolous white blossoms, and the sycamores seem to flex their knobby branches to appear otherworldly. It's a winter wonderland I don't get to see in ever-green Florida. Perfectly-shaped Tannenbäume festooned with white lights are set in containers along the sidewalk. Their piney scent infuses our path as we pass groups of happy people strolling, faces lit and free from care on this Saturday afternoon a week before Christmas. We walk. I talk. He nods.

No snow, but the air is frigid. Skies are overcast. In contrast to the brightly colored craft stalls, my father, cousin, and brother are dressed in black wool coats. I snap a photo and, when I look at it later, notice the uncompromising set of my brother's lips. Inwardly I sigh, knowing that it will take time. This is not a relationship that will be rushed. All I can do is be sincere and hope that he gets a sense of trust and forgiveness. Not just for me, though. He must forgive his father.

The Tower

Sulzbach
July 2017

I wander from the kitchen through the open doors to the front landing. I hear an insistent crowing, and now I see the proud cockerel as he struts into view inside the makeshift coop on the old town wall. He knows he is magnificent: a hefty specimen in white with black and gray sickle feathers, and a brilliant red comb with a wattle to match. As he promenades out of sight again, I see five dusty white hens follow. They scurry and bunch together with loud clucks while he moseys slowly along, confident of his posse. I will come to call this the daily strut.

I am spending two weeks at the Tower, a medieval construction of stone encased in the southwestern corner of the old town wall of Sulzbach-Rosenberg in Bavaria. The watchtower has been in my family for generations. I knew it best as the home of my Urgrosseltern, my great-grandparents, Martin and Anna. Vivid and abiding memories linger from ages four and five. After I left Germany with my mother and a new American father at age seven, I didn't return until I was twenty-eight, freshly divorced, and searching for redefinition in the heritage I had left behind. It would be many more years before I returned.

The Tower was constructed during the Middle Ages. Originally a watch tower, it became a powder tower before it was deemed useless and sold off to whomever wanted to make it habitable.

Far from luxurious, the Tower, with its massive stone walls, nevertheless provided a secure home. The original structure consisted of three floors of round rooms and a deep basement. The front door and lobby were later encased in a rectangular stucco addition that also held a kitchen and sitting room. A dizzying steep and twisty flight of stairs led to bedrooms on the second and third floors. The original arrow slits had been expanded into casement windows.

A small weathervane in the shape of a flag with a bold R was embedded on the turret roof above the large attic dormer window. Martin Renner had been raised here along with seven siblings, his parents, a cow, a goat, and a brood of chickens. Which may be why he was not in a big hurry to move back in. Although Martin inherited the Tower after his mother's death, his supervisor's job at the massive Maxhutte Steel Mill entitled him to a spacious flat in town, where he continued to live until his retirement. I assume it had a conveniently located washroom, one with heat and running water. Unlike the washroom in the Tower.

I remember that washroom well, even though I was probably six the last time I was in it. A tiny toilet room was tucked into a corner of the main floor, but the galvanized steel washtub fed by a sulfurous nearby spring was located deep in the unheated cellar. As a child when I visited my great-grandparents and had to take a bath, I fought it. The smell of sulfur steamed around me and clouded the dusty slat windows as I fervently prayed the devil was busy elsewhere until I was done being scrubbed down. Shivering from cold after being dried off, I would sprint back upstairs into the warmth and comfort of the kitchen.

•

Now I'm here at the Tower as a guest for two weeks. The town has deemed it an historic landmark and rents it out through their website. It's owned by family members I have yet to meet, Martin's grandson Erich and his wife Gabi. They are on holiday, and I hope to introduce myself when they return. In the meantime, I'm determined to dig into the Renner family history.

Someone once told me that the Tower had been bestowed upon my family for some worthy deed that no one could name. I figured the town archivist would have records. I found him in his office at the Stadtarchiv, seated at a room-length table piled high with dusty books and papers. More were stacked in corners like pillars.

Mr. Hartmann greeted me in rolled up jeans and a loose button-up shirt of russet colors to match his red hair. He pulled out paperwork and an old newspaper article which dated the Tower back to 1388. I told him that I had found history books with drawings at the town library which date from the 1500s. The Tower is depicted in all of them, like a proud sentinel. I asked him what noble deed had been done by great-great-grandpa to be granted such a gift.

His eyes widened, then crinkled with his smile. He shook his shaggy head. "I have paperwork that was signed in 1853, papers we have not been able to completely translate due to the old formal handwritten script. But it's clear the Tower was purchased by Leonhard, not bequeathed to him. It probably took a while to make it livable, especially for the winter. And there was a moat behind it that became a popular public swimming pool later."

When Leonhard bought it in 1853, he made the purchase as a twenty-nine-year-old single man. He agreed to pay 1,275 *guldens;* a currency used in the southern German regions at that time. (A good horse could be bought for about ten guldens). Leonhard made an initial down payment, then paid installments until he was handed an official certificate of ownership in 1868. During this time, he married a woman six years older and had three children with her before he died at the age of forty-five.

The pool was news to me, but I did remember a *Wäsherei*, a wash house that spanned a portion of what used to be a moat. My child's eyes saw heavy square beams, ancient and dark, above me, holding a tin roof, and below, icy water. The women would scrub the clothes with a brush, whack them against the beams in the water, and then drape them in the sunshine on the outer beams to dry. I scrabbled along the edge and collected a cache of errant shiny buttons which I kept in a glass jar.

Mr. Hartmann went on to explain that, after a string of noble owners, the castle grounds became a place of utility. When the last duke from the House of Wittelsbach left for a bigger city, Sulzbach needed money, so the town council decided to sell off unneeded portions. The old castle buildings now serve as a music school, and the town police station. Parts of the thick city wall were sold. Small houses of wood and stucco were built haphazardly on different sections of it.

My lusty rooster and his brood live on the wall, out of a blackened woodshed and adjoining open area that is enclosed with chicken wire and slopes down for about twenty feet. Below this, someone has hauled in soil and created a garden. A young couple with two children come to weed and water. The girl, who looks about four or five, runs around touching and talking to the lettuce and whatever else is planted. A wooden slat fence keeps her from tumbling off a drop of about fifteen feet onto the cobblestone street below.

Above and to the right of the chicken shed is another wood structure burnished by age, a narrow home with two dusty front windows. Two older men appear to live here. I see them make their way slowly down the steps in the morning, one stooped and shuffling, the other tall and erect with a long, gray ponytail. They dawdle the day away at a slatted picnic table, drinking beer, smoking, and cackling as they play cards. I wonder if they are the keepers of the rooster and his ladies. Above them is a two-story stucco house with a half tower attached. Today, snow-white bedcovers hang from an open window.

The town itself sits on a huge rock; everything is uphill and downhill. The downtown is flanked by two magnificent churches: one end is Catholic and the other Evangelical Lutheran. Both cast shadows over the cobblestone streets. Grüß Gott, a greeting that is meant as good day but which translates literally into "God greet you" rings out whenever folks pass each other.

My Aunt Sieglinde lives in the upper part of town. I hear the squeak of the front gate and stand up from my working perch at the kitchen table to see her march through the herb and rose garden. She bounds up ten steps to the open front door, brushes away an ivy tendril from the overgrowth on the front wall.

"Hallo, *Madlen*!" Sieglinde is here to help me wade through questions about the family. She gets distracted by the crowing of the rooster.

"*Ach*, that would drive me crazy! He is full of himself. Look! Look at his waltz!"

Sure enough, as we stand and walk outside, he's prancing in a semicircle, one wing extended to the ground. He sweeps it back and forth, and once again. His harem scatter to huddle in the corner by the shed. My aunt laughs.

"He is reminding his girls that he is the man here. So typical! See, he only has five hens. A healthy rooster is better off with about ten. He's probably wearing those girls out!" She laughs at my expression as unwanted images floated through my mind. Of dominance and chicken sex.

"It's okay," my aunt assures me. "The rooster protects the henhouse, keeps a look-out for danger. He waltzes to show them he is on the job. In return, he gets to do what nature intended."

My thoughts jump, unbidden, to my mother and her eventual acceptance of becoming a wife and mother. She was already thirty when she agreed to marry Ted, after years of insisting she never would give up her freedom. He offered her safety, and in return she gave him the children he wanted.

In 1961, my mother left Germany behind with a huge sigh of relief. The country was still rebuilding after the devastation of WWII, and America looked like the Promised Land. Mom didn't talk about either side of her family much. It is Sieglinde who now breaks the Renner history into fragments that I have to rejoin to create a new whole.

I had always thought that the loving great-grandmother I knew as a child was the mother of my grandmother Katharina, her two sisters and one brother. But Sieglinde shakes her head, purses her lips and taps my notebook. Looks at me with piercing blue eyes. "Here is where you can tell the truth, so everyone can understand why this side of the family is so distant."

She continues.

"No, no … the Uroma you knew was the stepmother, Anna. The mother of the children, Kathe, died when Anneliese, the youngest, was only five. When she passed, Martin married Anna. Fairly quickly. He needed help with the two youngest, especially Anneliese. But it backfired. Anneliese refused to accept the new mother and in turn, her stepmother was cold and demanding—like the stepmothers in fairy tales. It was terrible. The family became fragmented and sad. Anneliese never married. She didn't think she was lovable. Perhaps she blamed herself for her mother's poor health and decline. She spent her life as a teacher, very kind and supportive to her students. They were the family she never had."

My great-grandmother was thirty-nine when she had my Oma's youngest sister, Anneliese. The story is that she never completely recovered from the birth. Often bedridden, she suffered from various ailments and a malaise that eventually took her life at the age of forty-four. In the old photo album I have, her obituary is heavy with sorrow. The beautiful words penned by Martin called her *his loyal partner, her death tragic after a lifetime of deep and intense love. That she was leaving behind those who needed her, because God saw her need and pulled her to him.*

A curious thing happened a few months later: Martin posted an ad for a new wife. When Sieglinde told me this, I looked at her in shock. Really? Where, the local paper? Flyers posted in the local shops? WIDOWER WITH FOUR CHILDREN SEEKS NEW WIFE. OFFERS A MEDIEVAL TOWER AND A BEREFT FIVE-YEAR-OLD. Or something like that? Sieglinde wasn't certain, but yes, something like that.

Anna Koch responded. Photos of her depict a well-dressed matronly woman with an assuming air. She had spent many years in Switzerland as a nanny for a wealthy family and spoke fluent French. The faces of the great-grandparents I knew drift hazily into my mind's eye: short, robust bodies with ram-rod straight postures, prominent noses, and kind eyes. They could have been related. I hope they fell in love.

Martin hoped his new wife would be a loving mother to his five-year-old little girl. But it turns out Anneliese didn't take to the step-mother. She tried to shut her out. Told her father to get rid of her. Instead of trying to win the little girl over, Anna treated her harshly. During this time, the older children found ways to leave home in apprenticeship programs: Johann as a locomotive engineer, Susanne at a deaconess home. Katharina married Felix and moved away.

•

For me as a five-year-old, the Tower was a living fairy tale. A kitchen and cozy living area had been built out in front of the original stone edifice. This room was where all important things happened: warm hugs and warm food, quiet conversations and childish giggles. I delighted in my great-grandparents. At Christmas one year, I cut shiny star shapes from red and gold foil. I still have them; they grace my tree every year, although they are a bit tattered. The original structure was one round room on each of three floors, connected with impossibly narrow and winding steps with a heavy jute rope to hang on to. More twisty steps led to the attic, bedecked with intricate cobwebs and red dust from the roof tiles.

I would demand the very upstairs bedroom and curl up on the straw-tick mattress to stare at the ceiling and feed my romantic, my childish imagination. Here, Rapunzel combed her hair and waited patiently for her prince. When I walked out on the front landing, I always looked up at the dormer window and imagined long flaxen hair reaching towards the ground. How I envied her!

For I knew—without doubt—that he would come. The witch who had imprisoned her was powerless to his charms and strength. The prince was her protector. Did Anneliese also sleep on the straw-tick mattress, wishing and willing for a prince to show? Did she gaze out of the window onto the lush lawn below, with hope in her heart and a prayer on her lips? As a child, was I also waiting for my protector, sitting at the kitchen window with no long flaxen hair to offer? With only my strong desire to have a father in my life?

Knowing You, Knowing Me

Bad Nauheim
July 2017

A month to immerse myself in German life. A vacation rental with a spacious bedroom, combined living area with a small kitchen and a large Ikea kitchen table. A bathroom with a small shower; I can't bend over to shave my legs without my ass slapping the tile behind me. Banks of turn-and-tilt windows in all three rooms for maximum light and air flow. A small stone terrace that a bushy-tailed red squirrel and two fat blue jays call home. A charming place to have a light supper of sliced red peppers, cucumber, melon, and a fresh roll slathered with *quark*—cheese yogurt—beside a piece of salmon.

A month to get to know my father.

A year ago, I rang his bell. When I returned for his ninetieth birthday bash in December, our time was filled with festivities: Weinachstmärkte gawking, Glühwein drinking, Bratwurst eating, and a lot of oohing and aahing. This summer is our time to just hang out. To get to know each other in quiet times. Hopefully, there will also be time to spend with my new brother. Time to talk again. Time to find a definition for our relationship that we can both embrace.

The trip is topped off with a visit from my son, Jay. He will be joining me in a week to meet his Opa and spend time with his new extended family. Then he and I will fly the few hours to Iceland. In 2016, we stayed in Reykjavik, drove the Golden Circle, then over to the southern part to see the black sand beaches at Vik. We loved the island so much, we dreamed about going back to Akureyri in the north, where the landscape is completely different. It was after that 2016 trip with him that I went to Germany and found my father. This time, we'll do the same trip—Iceland, Germany—but in reverse, and like I introduced myself to my father, I'll be introducing my son to his grandfather.

My apartment is in a quiet residential neighborhood close to the forest with its many trails. I've rented a bicycle. It's a five-minute downhill ride to Father's apartment, three minutes to the town center, a minute to a narrow, paved walkway that cuts through to the numerous forest trails. If I want, I can ride up to Johannesburg, the small mountain whose ridge offers an excellent restaurant and an even better view of the town, the countryside, and the castle of Friedberg nearby. I attempted the uphill climb one morning but quickly gave up. I'm a flat-Florida girl. Today a ride into the woods took me past a mini farm with two colossal pigs mired in mud. Dusty hens pecked and clucked around the ankles of a middle-aged woman with blonde hair, rugged skin, and a quick smile.

Beyond her chain link fence lies a plateau of blue-green wheat. On the gravel path through the Hochwald, dense woodland on each side is carpeted in forest detritus. A slight downhill curve leads to adjacent ponds. Each one is graced with age-old willow trees weeping out over the water, trunks laced with moss. As I stood on the narrow plank bridge between them, small waterfowl strode on the thick mat of pond leaves, occasionally dipping their black heads into the murky water. In the adjacent pond, large fish appear out of the gloom only to vanish into the shadows of the weeping willow. A placard erected in front of the pond suggested I may be looking at a muddy catfish. Charcoal clouds hovered in the distance. A hut, its wood blackened with age, contained two benches waiting for those who may need to get out of the rain.

Later that afternoon, Papa, Niklas, and I were having coffee at an outdoor café called the Hexe Hütte, the Witches Hut. As we watched children splash in the small neighboring water park, thunder clapped loud and close. Some of the children screamed. A dog asleep underneath the next table bolted up, spun in circles and dove under its owners' feet. Niklas and I also jumped. My smiling father settled deeper into his chair. Puzzled at his lack of reaction, I looked at his ears. They were empty. Papa had left his hearing aids in the small bowl by his front door. Anni was not home when we left. She's the one who makes sure he has house keys, his wallet, hat, and sunglasses. She always tries to get him to take his walking stick, but most times he refuses. Anni keeps his life, and him, organized. He gratefully accepts this and anytime we start talking about making plans he tells me to get with her, happy to defer any large or small decision making.

Niklas and I gestured for him to finish his coffee, mimicking lifting the cup and drinking. Still sighing contentedly, he settled in even more, nodded at us and took a delicate sip. I pointed to the sky and the wind-tossed tree canopy. He looked up, and with a jolt told us that we needed to hurry, come on, let's go! Niklas looked at me and rolled his eyes. We were barely underway when the skies opened. What a sight we must have been: an old man, a, ahem, mature woman, and a burly young man dashing madly through parking lots and gardens. Home was only five minutes away, but on arrival we shook ourselves like wet dogs.

My dear Papa. He handed out towels; brought me an ironed, perfectly folded shirt of his. Hurried back into the bedroom. Now came a pair of his jogging pants, also freshly washed and pressed, (goodness, Anni must iron everything) which I declined. Niklas dried off and flounced onto the divan to turn on the television. I argued with my father about not messing up his perfectly ironed clothes. After the rain stopped, I hoofed it back to my flat and changed to return in time for *Abendbrot,* the traditional German evening meal of bread and cold cuts.

•

Time with my father has been rich and fluid. Initially in awe around him, I'm now comfortable and enjoy small moments in his company.

We've talked more about his relationship with Mom, although on this subject he remains a man of few words. I can tell he is reluctant, and careful, with what he says.

Ach, we were young. We wanted to have fun and took long rides on my motorcycle. We rode to Montabaur and I met her mother. We rode to Switzerland to see her sister Gunda, and then to Sulzbach to visit the Urgrosseltern … But things didn't work out, as you know. It was a time I put away, no need to dwell on things that can't be changed. I hope you understand.

I do.

He told me he's glad we're able to spend time together. I told him, me too.

There are challenges, of course. My command of German still isn't where I wish it to be. The grammar continues to be a bafflement to my Americanized brain. He has challenges, too. Often tells me he can't see, can't hear, his hands waving around his head like angry bees. Even with hearing aids in, gestures and loud repetitions are often necessary. But his energy is remarkable. I tend to forget his advanced age.

Our conversations are long and boisterous, words and phrases and gestures tossed about. Papa will find a marvelous word and pick it apart in English, German and French, understanding all its meanings and the nuances that may or may not be used interchangeably. He loves the sound of words, as do I. After learning the printing trade, my father began a long career in Germany's federal printing department, responsible for anything official such as banknotes, passports, and driver's licenses. He beams whenever we discuss books and my writing. His crowded shelves include German versions of some of my favorite books, including *Gone with the Wind* and *Rebecca*.

After the evening meal around seven, we often sit and chat as the insistent summer sun takes its slow leave. Tonight I mentioned Kant's *Das ding an sich* (a thing in itself); noumenon as opposed to phenomena: the thing that exists whether we recognize it or not. Thing. *Ding. Chose.* He went through his litany and then looked at me sternly: do you understand? It's impossible to fib, even when confession of not understanding will launch him into telling me the same thing in several different ways. For a man who claims not to see well, he is able to look intensely in my eyes to find truth.

I reminded him I don't speak French. He sighed, as if he were speaking to a child who had not done her lessons.

"*Chose.* It means a thing."

We switched to history. How everyone, even children, drank ale in the Middle Ages as an alternative to dirty water. We discussed an Arquebus—the first long gun—and the disadvantages of needing a tripod to hold it, which in turn led to the more mobile musket. I pulled up photos of the Tower in Sulzbach on my phone and pointed to the remaining unaltered arrow slits.

"Here you go. The bow and arrow came first. Then the poor guard had to figure out how to balance and aim the Arquebus through these tiny openings. Once he could use a musket his life, and aim, was better, right?"

He nodded sagely and looked pleased, as if I had learned something after all.

Our discussions typically become a lively roundabout of hand waving, pointing, arm touching, laughing, sighing, and Google Translate (which he calls that clever machine) between the three of us. Anni often understands my translations first and tells Papa, who cups his ear, then exclaims *ah* and repeats to confirm understanding, nodding wisely. The time we spend around the table, this warmth and comfort and ease; well, this is something I didn't have at home, not once, growing up.

It feels like family.

•

Papa, Anni, and I take the train from Bad Nauheim to Frankfurt Airport. Jay is on the non-stop flight from Orlando which gets in around 11:00 a.m. I've reserved Luka Taxi for the return to Bad Nauheim. My stomach is roiling with nerves. Will Jay like his Opa?

Will they be able to communicate well enough, since Jay doesn't understand German? I don't want their time together to be awkward. I've filled the next few days with walking activities that should take care of uncomfortable silences. My son will enjoy the blackthorn towers with their dissipating salty air and the rejuvenating Kneipp pool in the herb gardens. We have dinner planned at Tiramisu, my favorite Italian eatery close to our rental apartment.

As Jay appears at the exit with his duffel bag, my eyes well up and spill over. He looks tired and nervous. I grab him in a tight hug and hold on way too long. He shushes me and looks embarrassed. Heads toward my father with his arm outstretched for a handshake. His new Opa and Oma welcome him with big hugs and exclamations of delight, which serves for more embarrassment: here are three old people not able to control their emotions. My son hates a scene, and he looks for the door leading out to the taxis.

Luka is waiting and loads the duffel into the trunk. Anni and Walter will take the train back so Jay and I can catch up. We will get together again later in the afternoon for coffee.

•

My father has chronicled his life in photos and videos. Years of travel around the world are recorded, often in both stills and movement, then notated with a voice-over. Pages upon pages of detailed written description. As are events with friends and family. During our afternoon coffee at Müllers' Bakery, I looked back to find him with the video recorder held up to record my pastry selection. Each visit nets me a CD of our time together. He has also Googled my name and found my website, with all my writings and media. They have been printed out and sit in a folder with my name in large letters across the front.

When Jay and I get to the apartment around 4:00, my father falls into his favorite routine: sharing his life. Often in the afternoons he will open a cabinet, and with his index finger trail the spines of the binders of DVDs he has catalogued until he finds one he wants to share with me. He'll slip on a huge pair of magnifying goggles so he can see, headphones so he can hear, and inserts his choice into the DVD player. Then he settles in with a small smile. He looks over occasionally to make sure I'm delighted. I smile and nod. He wiggles his bottom into the chair and nods back, satisfied. Or we get out the photo albums so I can feast my eyes on a happy, healthy mother. Today we delve into the latter, and Jay gets to experience his grandmother as a happy young girl.

Birthdays, holidays, festival days, vacations; every year has been celebrated. Hair color, body weight, eyeglasses, and clothes, chronicle the changes as time rolled by. I have gotten to know my father's mother and sister, and their home in Frankfurt which was bombed twice during the Allied invasion. No photos of his father. He told me his parents divorced at the end of the war but did not elaborate. The final video of his sister Bertha shows her in a wheelchair on an outing in a park. She is gaunt, a far cry from the stout and smiling aunt who held me proudly for the camera when I was three. She died a few days after the recorded outing.

Papa continues to create a continuum of his existence. With camera or recorder in hand, he saves present moments for the future. He says he doesn't believe in God: "Because of the war—especially at the end of the war, when we found what people had done to each other—I knew there couldn't be a God. What matters is family." And this I know. Their small family has always been close, Oma and Opa happily involved in Niklas' upbringing. Birthdays and holidays celebrated with various aunts and uncles. When I commented on his diligence in recording the events in his life, he nodded. "I figure one day my memory may go. If it does, I can go back and know I existed."

Now my son will be part of those memories. The video camera began in the airport, recording our emotional greeting for posterity. My handsome manchild with the family blue eyes, once blonde cropped hair, and lush mahogany beard which Papa remarked on with a chuckle, something about the lack of razors in America and the Taliban. Today, he is treated to pictures of me as a child. I'm not so sure about his comfort level. Everything German is foreign to him, and he side-eyes me a few times, as if he is looking at a stranger. But he smiles politely, and eventually his shoulders ease as he feels the happiness in the room. Accepts that his mother is more than just his mother.

We meet my half-brother Michael and his family that night for dinner. The conversation flows, and I notice Jay assessing his cousin, Niklas. They share a similarity in looks, with a strong forehead and deep-set blue eyes. Both handsome. Both strong. They both tend to watch everything and keep opinions to themselves, making it difficult to know what they are thinking.

Later that night, back at our apartment, Jay mentions the similarity in looks that he and Niklas share. We end up discussing genetics, and the traits that run through him from multiple nationalities. My husband's paternal side is mostly English, originated from Anglo Saxons who were Germanic people from Northern Germany and Denmark. His maternal side, Hungarians, originated from Magyars, an ethnic group from central Russia who ultimately mingled with several races creating a diversity of skin and hair color. My genetics testing shows mostly German, along with a quarter Frankish, which also includes Germanic tribes.

Although we tend to look at physical features as a manifestation of genetics, so much more goes into family resemblance. My husband has dark brown hair and brown eyes; his mother was blonde and blue-eyed and his father had dark brown hair and brown eyes. Everyone in my German family had or has blue eyes, with blonde or brown hair; I have greenish-blue eyes and so does Jay. As a child, he looked like the perfect Aryan specimen, with light blonde hair and those blue eyes, but as he grew into adulthood his hair darkened.

I think about the children who were taken from their families in other countries to be "Germanized" because they met the physical criteria of what was considered desirable and superior. What would have happened to my son once his hair changed color?

•

Papa calls himself a pessimist, but I disagree. So does Anni. When he adamantly makes statements about the sorry state of people, the country, the world, she looks up at the ceiling and shakes her head, a smile playing at the corners of her mouth. In the next sentence, he will extol virtues of the very subject he just maligned. An understanding of the yin and yang inherent in all things. I would call him a pragmatist at worst, a realist at best. He's also gregarious. During our frequent outings, he loves to hobnob with folks nearby, which often leads to introductions and a promise to see each other again soon. He always introduces me as "meine Tochter aus Amerika." This never fails to get a raised eyebrow, and a curious eye turned on me.

There are moments in our conversations when his face clouds. If I ask a question about the war. Or sometimes about my childhood. There are memories and feelings he doesn't wish to share with me. Yet. Time may change that. Or perhaps these are things I don't need to know.

One day we were sitting over lunch, and I asked him how many times he was able to arrange a visit with me when I was a child. We had been talking about the video in which I showed off with the red scooter and the hula hoop. I was laughing at my frenetic need for attention, which was so obvious. He looked away for a moment, then looked down. His smile faded. I saw resignation and anger in his face. "Not often," he answered. Then he changed the subject.

He must have been devastated to be denied contact with his child. As a mother, I would find it impossible. At some time, at some point in my life, I heard that his family wanted to take me in, but my angry mother would not have it. I can't remember where or how I heard this. Or maybe it was wishful thinking.

For now, I must be satisfied with the time we spend in laughter and discovery. And self-discovery. What I have come to realize is the enormity of reference: of knowing who I am by knowing who my father is. A relief. To have only had my mother as a reference, allowing it to be tainted by all the shortcomings I heaped on her created a sense of incompleteness. We need our parents to reflect from, at least when we are children. Sure, sometime in early adolescence many of us decide we desperately need to be different than those odd and boring creatures we live with. But if we're lucky, a secure foundation has been laid that we can balance on. Not all of us get to feel that sense of security.

Throughout youth, into middle age—and even now if I let it—uncertainty has prevailed. The Thesaurus offers alternatives: anxiety, ambiguity, ambivalence, confusion, mistrust, skepticism, suspicion, disquiet, indecision, puzzlement, bewilderment. Can I admit that all those synonyms were mine to juggle at any given time? Yes. And the most defining? Lack of confidence. Whenever I tried to figure out why I felt uncertain, the answer that came to mind was that I was misplaced.

No amount of accomplishment, no amount of attention, nor profuse reassurances could quell the incessant restlessness I felt. I was that child who sits in the front row in school, frantically waving her hand when she knows an answer: pick me, pick me. Pick me so I can prove that I'm worthwhile. Important decisions created agony: was it the best one? It wasn't okay to be okay. I wanted so badly to excel. I wanted to turn the differences I felt into something extraordinary, because I never felt that I could be ordinary and be okay.

Until I saw the frenetic video of myself, I thought my uncertainty came from being plucked out of my native country and thrown into one so foreign that I was unable to adapt properly. I needed something and someone to blame, so I fixated on the severing of my German umbilical cord. Set adrift, I tapped first one foot and then the other, unable to find solid purchase. I blamed my mother because she made those choices for me.

But since spending time with Papa, I believe the uncertainty is rooted in early childhood. When I think I have disappointed someone I care deeply for, let them down in some way, my heart seizes before it gallops crazily. Synapses in my brain flash and ignite. I can't breathe. The guilt is sometimes overwhelming. Should I assume this was ingrained in that child who thought only of herself, callously unresponsive to her grandmother's wishes to stay out of trouble and harm? A desire for control over my life lies at the heart of it all.

Mom told me a story about one of my shenanigans, as was told to her by Oma. This makes the veracity iffy at best since the facts have been rearranged in multiple memories multiple times. But as I listened to it, images and smells flooded in, along with my thoughts.

The child is lounging on the kitchen divan, it's afternoon nap time—during which naps rarely occurred—when she sits up. Quietly makes her way out of the apartment door, down two flights of freshly waxed mahogany stairs, out the front door, down the sidewalk, across Kantstrasse, and somehow makes her way to the four-lane highway on which cars zip past on the exit road into the town of Montabaur. The police officer who brings her home explains to her shocked Oma that she was found in the middle of the highway, arms flailing first in one direction, then another. Very much as if she were attempting to direct traffic.

My intentions are unclear as I recall my route to the highway. But the streets I crossed, the asparagus growing along the highway and the sound of the cars zipping by are there. Perhaps I wasn't in the middle of the highway, perhaps I was off to the side, in the midst of the wild asparagus. If I were to venture a guess as to motivation, it's possible that my almost constant uncertainty translated into an immense need for action, for a sense of control. Was this prompted by the father who came and went, a mother who appeared and disappeared? Or by the grandmother who, after raising six children of her own, was handed a responsibility she hadn't asked for?

My mother raised me with criticism. I realize now that she may not have known another way to show her concern. The way her life was as a child, with her mother's need to rely on her at much too tender an age, may have rendered her incapable of giving loving support. Her attempts to guide me translated into *do not do this, or that bad thing will happen*. It is my mother's life, her fears, that she passed on to me. The stress on Oma to work and provide for six children must have been tremendous. My mother carried the brunt of day-to-day household chores and care for her siblings. One of her greatest fears must have been to fall short of what was expected of her. There was also the specter of legal ramifications. Rules were a way of life, and a breach could bring about a heavy knock on the door, a lack of rations, or worse.

One clear memory stands out. I was sixteen and hung out with a group, mostly boys, in the first neighborhood we moved to in Florida after Ted retired from the Army. We skipped school occasionally, got high on pot, and caused neighborhood mayhem now and then. One night we found an unoccupied house with a pool and decided to go skinny-dipping. When we finished, we threw all the patio furniture into the pool. As we made our way out, bright lights and three police cars waited for us. Fortunately, we were taken home, our parents informed that, next time, they would have to come to the police station to bail us out. I was put on restriction. My stepfather was livid. When Mom looked at me I saw fear in her eyes. She pleaded, something like: "Please stay out of trouble until you're eighteen. Then you won't be my responsibility anymore."

I can't help but wonder about the person I would be had my life been guided by the strong confidence of the father I am coming to know. He is a man of character and high morals. He's loving and understanding. I can only guess at what he was like as a younger man. Perhaps I'm romanticizing. But now, finally, in the encroaching golden years of life, there is hope and a true possibility of belonging. Of fitting my odd-shaped sockets into the proper slots to complete the puzzle picture. With no shadow of insecurity lurking about.

One thing I was certain of when my son was born: he will be raised in a home of security and love, with every opportunity to be the person he is meant to be. I never want him to feel as if a part of him is missing or dismissed, like I did. The days we spend with Papa and Anni, brother Michael and his family, slide by with ease and enjoyment. As I look back on this trip, I know it became the beautiful and secure bow of the knot that ties us together as family.

Channeling Elvis

Bad Nauheim
October 2017

I am immersed in a deep wooden tub touted to be over a hundred years old. Staring down at me with come-hither smoldering eyes and his signature sexy sneer is Elvis Presley. I stare down at my naked body cradled in briny water and fight a desire to cover myself with the miniscule white square of washcloth I'm gripping. Steam radiates upward in tiny tufts. I push down on the sides of the tub until only my face is out of the water. I wonder if Elvis actually reclined in this very tub or if someone's shrewd marketing decided that peppering the room with his photos would qualify this particular cubicle as The Elvis Bathhouse. I wonder if Anni paid extra for this special room.

I shift, push my back against the tub and squirm to find that spot that will numb the pain. Water splashes onto the marble floor. Healing spring water is being pumped into Badehaus #3 from the magnificent Art Nouveau fountain outside. The Empress Auguste Viktoria, wife of Wilhelm II, frequented the bathhouse from 1881 until the fall of the Prussian Empire and end of WWI in 1918. I'm not aware of a room named after her, though.

I'm in Bad Nauheim again to visit with Papa and Anni, but this trip has turned into a nightmare. I feel like a burden instead of a welcome visitor. Anni booked a bath for me as another attempt to relieve the chronic and debilitating pain I've had since a week after my arrival on October 18th. I close my eyes and drift, remembering.

•

Arrival
October 2017

I disembark Lufthansa flight LH465 stiff, dry-eyed, and dry-mouthed after eight and a half hours in the air. The overnight flight isn't conducive to sleep; too many restless bodies trying to find comfortable positions. I chose this flight because it's nonstop. On this trip I plan to spend a few days in Bad Nauheim to hang out with my father, then a few days with cousin Michael and Ivonne before driving down to the Tower in Sulzbach to visit Aunt Sieglinde. Then back to Bad Nauheim for a week before flying home. A grand plan to see those I love.

Customs is always the same:" Why are you here?" I'm asked by a young, handsome German man. Eyes narrow a bit as he looks at me, his poker face assessing. I tell him in German that my family lives here. "Oh? Where?"

"All over. My father lives in Bad Nauheim."

"Oh? You're German?" He squints at my passport, which clearly states I'm American. They notice the place of birth, Bad Homburg, a town just outside of Frankfurt.

"Yes. My mother married an American." Ah ha. Now the mystery is solved. They wave me through. I smile: "Einen schönen Tag noch!"

Today is the first time my cousin Michael isn't here to greet me as I pass through the final secure area. So far Michael has been my chauffeur, interpreter, and hand holder as I rediscover my father. But this trip I'm determined to function independently. I've been working on my German with online classes.

I head to the car rental kiosks and find Sixt.

"Reservierung für Lock," I begin in German.

A well-dressed young lady behind the counter swivels around, gives me an appraising look and answers in English. "How was your flight?"

Inwardly I sigh and switch to English as well. "As pleasant as sitting up all night can be." I give a bark of laughter.

The rental is a fire-engine red Fiat. I play with the navigation system and plug in the address of my hotel in Bad Nauheim. Ease down the curvy garage exit and hit sunlight. Deep breath and I'm on my way. Nervous fingers tap the wheel as I accelerate onto the autobahn. The car jumps like a greyhound into a race. Remember the rules: don't pass on the right; watch out for speed limits (yes, there are some, sporadically); before passing on the left, check way down the road—someone driving 120 kilometers per hour will be on you in a second.

Thirty minutes later, I pull up in front of Hotel Spöttel, a ten-minute walk from Papa's flat. My nerves are prickling. I need sleep before seeing Papa and Anni. A quick shower and I climb between soft sheets, float into a fast sleep. Until my head begins buzzing, a persistent insect inside my brain. It's the front desk letting me know my father is in the front parlor. Oh. I vacillate between exhaustion and excitement, pull on jeans and a sweater, and clomp down three floors. Afternoon sun floods the elegant staircase and stabs at my weary eyes.

My Papa, legs splayed, is standing in the sunshine coming through a large picture window in the antique-filled reception lounge. He has on a Russian fur cap and a black wool coat. "*Na ja, meine Tochter*," he says as he reaches for a hug. It's only been early August since I've seen him, but it feels like an overdue homecoming. I tell him I'll come down to his flat in an hour, after a change of clothes and a strong cup of espresso. I'm giddy about spending the next four days with him, walking the glorious parks, and drinking afternoon coffee, while we continue to discover each other.

The days fly by. We walk, gulp crisp air, drink perfect coffee, and laugh a lot. The morning I'm to leave for Neustadt to visit Michael, I haul two suitcases down to the lobby with the help of an ancient lift. I wheel them over to reception to settle my bill. As I turn to leave, my left knee doesn't turn with me. Intense pain and a quick glance confirm I have wrenched the kneecap out of position. On the bad knee. The one that already had two surgeries for a torn ligament from a bad ski fall a few years ago while visiting Jackie in Colorado with my son. I ignored my injuries after that fall, until I tore my meniscus while twisting my leg getting into my car, and ended up with a double surgery.

I hobble into the lobby and wrench it back to where it sort-of should be. I can put some weight on it, but it's already beginning to swell. Not thinking clearly, I wrestle the luggage to the car and begin the hour-and-a-half drive to Neustadt. By the time I arrive, the useless knee is stiff and swollen, throbbing a steady beat which tandems into my skull. Ivonne clucks around me, concerned and helpful. Ice. Ibuprofen. Elevation. The care that should have happened immediately.

The next day it's no better, and she calls her orthopedist who slides me in. X-rays show some fluid cradling my arthritic patella. Dr. Steinbaugh determines a mild strain and assures me it will heal—he gives me a steroid shot, a script for 600mg ibuprofen and tells me to stay off the knee for five days. This means I must change plans to drive to Sulzbach in two days to stay at the Tower and spend time with Sieglinde. I had also planned to finally meet Gabi Renner. She is the widow of Erich Renner, the son of Oma's brother Johann. Erich died last year of a prolonged illness.

I decide to postpone my stay at the Tower until the end of my visit, in two weeks. This should give my knee time to heal. I'll stay at Michael's for the next few days and return to Bad Nauheim once I get clearance to drive. In the meantime, I have lots of time to ponder on things while sitting at the kitchen table with my knee propped up. Ivonne works at an after-school program at the local elementary. She had asked me to give a reading of *Ethel the Backyard Dog*, the children's book I wrote and published a few years ago. We've decided to postpone that, too.

I sit and doodle notes on a legal pad while I think about the twists and turns my life has taken this last year. I want to see Sieglinde and let her tell me more about her life. I want to ask her how she has coped so positively with the knowledge of her existence and who her father was. Also, her darkest moments. Her faith has been the bedrock for acceptance of who she is, how she came into the world. God had a purpose for her life. But never the nunnery, she says. She knew she was meant to be a wife and mother. To nurture.

The desire to share her secret in that small café years ago was prompted by her need to be a witness. Dark moments must have followed the confession. Why now, she may have thought. Much like my father's family must have thought—why now, after all this time, do I show up on their doorstep? But I do know I have to get both our stories right. To look at them from all angles and try to understand the motivations behind the actions. Not only for my Oma Katharina but also for my mother. It makes my head hurt to stay open-minded, to let judgement drop so I can see as much of the truth as is possible.

Frustration at my bad knee and limited movement gnaws away at me; I'm a burden for Ivonne. After lolling around for three days I get clearance to drive. But not to Sulzbach where my thoughts have been. It's a three-hour ride on the autobahn. Instead, I drive the hour or so back to Father's town. Waving cheerfully to Michael and Ivonne, I carefully engage the clutch and find acceptance in a healing knee. I wind the Fiat through the narrow streets of Michael's town. Gaze longingly at the acres and acres of vineyards, the stocks now grape-less and bright in their yellow and red autumn mantles. Soon, they will be cut back to prepare for next year's harvest. If not for this injury, I would have spent hours biking or hiking the utility roads that crisscross the fields. *Next time* I whisper. And cut onto the exit for the autobahn, headed for Bad Nauheim.

Papa is delighted I'm back. With a still tender knee, our long walks shuffling through shifting carpets of russet and yellow leaves are out. I'm only able to hobble. Father decides it's a good time to take a tour of Frankfurt on the *Ebbel-wei Express.* In late 1970, two local artists were commissioned to transform an ordinary tram car into an apple-wine pub on wheels. It's decorated with local points of interest and specialties, including a large Lebkuchen heart and Martin Luther in his floppy hat. With Papa and Anni, brother Michael, and seventeen-year-old Niklas, we climb aboard and settle in our seats.

For an hour we circle the city while polka music blares over a scratchy sound system. We sip apple wine, crunch pretzels, and gaze up at the tall skyscrapers of this major world financial hub. We cruise past Römerberg Square, which was once considered the most beautiful in the German nation. It is located opposite the Römer building complex, which has been the seat of the city administration since the fifteenth century. Much of Frankfurt's Altstadt offers reconstructed history since the city was bombed to rubble in WWII, but the architecture here remains a witness.

After a quick peek at Goethe's home, we end up at Pizza Hut. Lunch is a deep-dish pie. Since I'm not able to walk along the historic River Main, we climb back into the car for the forty-minute ride back to my brother's house, where his wife Bettina will have coffee and waffles waiting for us.

Papa and Anni make sure that we get together with my brother and his family whenever I visit. Usually we go out for dinner, but today we have been invited to their villa, located in the next town over from Bad Nauheim. Bettina has made Herzwaffeln, those heart-shaped sweet waffles that are a German specialty. The dining table is a pretty tableau of fine china on a white linen tablecloth, and three cut crystal bowls: one filled with a mound of home-made sahne—a light whipped cream—another with powder sugar, and yet one more with fresh berries. A pot of fresh coffee sits in the middle. A feast for the eyes as well as the taste buds.

I feel the ease as we chat about the day. I compliment Bettina on her beautiful table and delicious food. Hope blossoms in me for a chance at full acceptance. Gone are the quick covert glances of assessment. Instead I see trust blossoming. Not all the way there yet, but certainly on the right path. I feel a bubble of happiness and sink back into my seat.

By the time Papa, Anni, and I are ready to go, I sense a tightness mid-back, right side. I've probably been compensating for that damn left knee, shifting my weight to ease off it. I can't wait to call it a night and crawl into a soft bed at what is dubbed the Elvis Presley hotel.

Villa Grunewald is a small yet architecturally opulent hotel that hosted Private Presley when he was stationed nearby from 1958 to 1960. At that time, Germany was overrun with American troops, the terms of WWII augmented by the impending Cold War. Some small towns had as many troops as residents. Barracks and bases were thrown up.

Elvis climbed off the troop transport carrier USS General George M. Randall in Bremerhaven along with 1,169 other soldiers, and arrived by jeep in Friedberg, about two miles south of Bad Nauheim. His celebrity took precedence over any outrage much of the German citizenry felt at this invasion. Elvis posed for pictures, signed autographs, and participated in PR events. He recorded an old German folk song in English and German, *A Wooden Heart.* All over the country, *Fräulein* swooned. American military boys suddenly found themselves popular under Elvis's lore.

Today a black granite stele sits just outside the hotel gate with a white marble relief of The King on it. At its base are colorful piles of flowers, stuffed bears, love letters and photographs from visiting fans. The European Elvis Festival takes place in August, covering a weekend close to the sixteenth, the date of his death.

But that's not my reason for staying here. It was, simply, affordable and one block from the main town center. I don't request #10, The King's room. What I get is a tiny room with nondescript black modern furniture. The downstairs bistro serves good wine and better flammkuchen, a local specialty made with a super thin crispy crust and layered with crème fraiche, along with whatever else the kitchen has to offer.

For the first time in months, I sleep through the night and awaken as gray light floods through the sheer curtains. When I sit up to check the time, I scream. Someone has taken a handful of stilettos (knives, not shoes) and rammed them into my right scapula. I climb out of bed and the pain intensifies. My right arm is almost numb. After a few minutes I am hyperventilating. I manage to pull on jeans and stumble downstairs to reception. An efficient looking young woman does her best to understand my histrionics and promises to find a doctor.

"Please madam, go back up and lie down."

It's not long before she softly knocks on the door and tells me she's found a Chinese doctor a five-minute walk away. *Can I go now, please?* She gives me directions—Dr. Wang is located next to Tegut, a small grocery store on the main street. *Yes, I know where it is.* I hurry out. Dr. Wang is waiting for me. Her office isn't open yet, but she wants to help. Her eyes fill with concern as she waves me into a large exam room. A few minutes later, I look like a porcupine. And the pain is gone.

Oh, blessed relief. I lie on a long table, gulping deep pockets of air while my heart rate returns to normal. I drift away, to wake up with her shiny black eyes a few inches from mine. She touches different areas on my back and neck. "Tut es weh?" And again, over and over, "Tut es weh?" Does it hurt? No and no. She pulls the acupuncture needles out and I tentatively sit up. So far so good. For about three minutes. By the time I'm dressed and she's calculating my bill, the pain is back. I sit down in tears.

Dr. Wang, alarmed and determined, ushers me back into the exam room, pulls out a multi-armed contraption with glass cups and a movement of its own that makes me think for one horrific moment of an attacking octopus. I think it must be cupping, but I don't understand what she's saying. Our exchange in three languages doesn't work so well. It doesn't matter; the suction takes away the pain again. I drift and breathe. When Dr. Wang returns, we admire the purple marks decorating me. She carefully removes the cups. The pain hovers but maintains a respectful distance. We schedule another acupuncture session for the next day. By the time I return to Villa Grunewald, the pain is back full force. I climb into bed, sobbing.

If I lie flat on my back and push into the mattress, neck tucked, it seems to numb the source of pain. I cradle my cellphone and call Anni and Papa. They rush over. Anni comes armed with arnica cream and paracetamol. She makes sympathetic noises and calls my father's orthopedic. Since I'm not part of the German health system, I have to go as a private cash patient. These are only accepted at certain times on certain days. Fortunately, I'm only a day out.

In the meantime, Anni thinks a Thai massage may help and calls for an appointment. Poor Papa keeps shaking his head. They both speculate on what brought this on, and I try to explain that my spine is in bad shape, with several vertebrae sitting bone on bone. This flare-up is surely an accumulation of walking in the wrong kind of boots and not stretching enough. At home I do yoga several times a week, which helps.

In the next eight days, I will see four more doctors: three orthopedists and one hapless intern at Hochwald Hospital emergency room, along with Dr. Wang. One doctor writes me a prescription for 600 milligrams of ibuprofen, cautioning me to take one in the morning with breakfast and one in the evening with dinner. Another prescribes Tilidine (turns out to be a type of opioid painkiller which did not do much) and an ointment. Nothing seems to help, not even the Elvis bathhouse. I end up mostly bedridden and miserable. Anni and poor Papa are beside themselves and check on me several times a day.

A few days later, I convince Anni to drive me to the emergency room in the evening, hoping for a pain shot so I can sleep the night. It's closed until nine. while the one attending intern is on his break. We pace while we wait. Up and down the hallway we go. I'm grimacing in pain. Father trails me with his hands clasped behind his back, shaking his head. I feel miserable about making them feel miserable.

Anni stays calm and practical, which seems to be her natural demeanor. Unlike my mother who always seemed to run on emotion. Mom would have spent her time chastising me for not taking care of myself better: I should have known not to traipse all over town in pretty boots with heels. And she would have been right, but it also would have been the last thing I needed. Of course, Anni isn't my mother and isn't inclined to speak her mind to me. But I feel so much better with her at the helm.

A young studious-looking man in white scrubs appears and unlocks the ER door. I explain the situation. He gives me a shot of clear liquid which I assume is morphine. Although the shot takes the edge off the pain for a few hours, it is back full force the next morning.

I feel like a useless mound of flesh and my mind can't focus on a single rational thought. I give in to it and lay in bed all day, under the non-influence of drugs that don't work, listening to audio books: *Why Buddhism is True* by Robert Wright, Steinbeck's *Grapes of Wrath*, Mary Shelley's *Frankenstein*. Kind Anni comes in the mornings and evenings to rub arnica onto my shoulder and back and makes sure I get something to eat from the downstairs bistro. A few times I hobble downstairs to sit in the lobby with Papa, but all he can do is look as helpless as I do.

The pain eases when I lay on my left side and position my right arm straight over my head. This also helps sitting or walking, which garners me alarmed looks whenever I wander out of my room and encounter another guest. Or perhaps it's the way I look, with unwashed hair, no makeup and a frightening frown of disbelief at no relief. I spend the days before I finally leave for home mostly in bed hoping that I recover enough to spend ten hours in the air. I try to get a business-class ticket with no luck. On the day I leave, three weeks after arriving, I take two diazepam and fight nausea on the way to the airport. Memory now can't conjure up the check-in, or the flight.

This trip showed me at my worst; the pain made me cranky. Yet my newfound family rallied. Father and Anni went out of their way to make sure I had meals every day and offered as much comfort as was possible. The time spent with my brother was another step toward acceptance. Although he is more relaxed, he continues to absorb the fact that he now has a half-sister.

•

November again … later.

When I finally arrive home and get to an urgent care center, a CAT scan reveals I have cervical radiculopathy, compressed nerves in my neck. After a powerful cocktail of morphine and steroids, the pain finally leaves. I'm referred to a neurosurgeon, get an MRI, and can now see clearly that three vertebrae in my neck are bone on bone. Two of these have grabbed a few important nerves heading into my right arm. I am told I may never regain full use of my right hand. Devastated and pain weary, I dive into melancholy. My right arm and hand are useless.

While I wait for a follow-up appointment with the neurosurgeon and a call from a pain specialist to schedule (two weeks out, soonest available) I heal. One morning, I get up and my arm functions. No numbness, no pain. When I research online, I read that, often, radiculopathy resolves itself in six weeks to three months. I glance at the calendar: today is right at six weeks. Slowly and carefully, I ease back into yoga. I stay off the computer a while longer. I learn to walk on the balls of my feet. I baby myself. I plan the next trip to Germany for the summer and determine to keep myself healthy. And buy good walking shoes.

The Elvis Bathhouse

The Belt

Journal
Florida, 2018

Back in 1983, Mom, Jackie, and I flew home to reconnect with family. Jackie had never been to Germany. I had not been there since I left at the age of seven. Our relatives were getting older and my mother said it was time to go home. We stayed with Aunt Christel in Remscheid, located in the mid-western part of the country. She and her husband became our guides. We made day trips to Cologne to visit Aunt Erika, drove into bucolic Switzerland to visit Aunt Gunda, and down into Bavaria to visit Aunt Sieglinde, where we stayed at the Tower.

Then, the stone sentinel was still furnished with musty old things from Martin and Anna. Jackie and I grabbed the very top, round room. Two straw-tick mattresses in single wooden bed frames rustled like dry leaves as we squirmed to get comfortable at night. A heavy maple armoire and a nightstand that was dwarfed under a Delft wash basin and pitcher completed the décor. The closest toilet was three flights down steep winding steps. A pitted white enamel chamber pot sat between the two beds for nighttime peeing.

The ancient attic lay directly above our ceiling. Early one morning, I woke up thinking about treasures that may be jumbled in old boxes, covered with tiny mouse turds, and sending out whispers of wishes to be discovered. Sliding as lightly as possible out of bed, I glanced at Jackie's tousled blonde hair as she slept on, and tip-toed out of the bedroom onto the landing to stare up at the attic steps. An old hemp rope functioned as a railing. A massive rusty hook latched a trap door. I wrestled it open and pushed through cobwebs and dust motes. Hoping to find boxes of letters and photos, pieces of furniture and old clothing, imagine my disappointment when, except for a few old empty cardboard boxes and a small broken picture frame, I found the room empty of mementos.

Broken adobe roof tiles were piled under a dormer window. I thought a few pieces could serve as a keepsake to take home and began digging through the stack. There, close by and tucked into an opening, was the belt. Memory serves a tricky truth, and I can't recall my thoughts at that time. Perhaps the buckle frightened me, the swastika so bold, the eagle intimidating with its spread wings and claws grasping the circle of thorns. Perhaps I felt it was valuable. Probably, selfishly, I wanted it to be mine and worried about having to give it up. I scuttled back down to our room to nestle it inside my suitcase.

When I returned to Florida, I buried it deep in a chest of personal items, where it remained. I was twenty-eight, finishing up a BA in English Lit at the University of South Florida. Life got busy and I didn't think about the belt or my family history much. The small chest of personal items traveled with me as I moved in and out of various apartments, and finally into the home where I now sit in front of the computer.

Sieglinde's revelation and the discovery of Oma's secrets have ignited the memory of the belt and questions are pelting me. Who did it belong to? What does it mean? Who hid it and why? Is there still someone living that can answer, or is the truth lost to history? I stare at the image on the computer screen, then back at the belt coiled like a viper on my desk. I pick it up and hold it next to the color photo. There's no doubt it's a perfect match: the symbol is for the Sturmabteilung, the SA. The brass of the buckle is pitted and tarnished, but the insignia is perfectly preserved: a beaded circle encompasses an eagle, wings spread wide, clutching a wreathed sunwheel encircled in oak leaf trim with piped borders. In the middle sits a swastika, the Hakenkreuz.

I wonder how the swastika became a symbol of hatred and discrimination and do more research. The Sanskrit *Svastika* translates into *that which is associated with well-being*: *Su-* good, well; *Asti,* to be; *ka* functions as a diminutive, or intensifier. This symbol of good luck had been used for at least 5,000 years in many Eastern religions, including Buddhism and Hinduism. It made its way onto artifacts of pre-Christian Europe. Some were even found on Byzantine and Christian art and architecture.

The connection between the ancient Aryan race and the Swastika erupted from the work of Heinrich Schliemann, a German archeologist. In 1871, he continued excavations begun by the British archeologist Frank Calvert, at a site called the Hisarlik Mound. It ended up being the city of Troy. Schliemann took the lion's share of credit for the discovery. What he also uncovered were over 1,800 variations of the swastika, most of them on pottery shards. He brought the symbol home. To Hitler and the Nazis. The swastika became the Hakenkreuz.

Fine hairs on my neck prickle as my heart begins to gallop. Grandpa Felix, and any other male in the family aged sixteen and up had served time in the Wehrmacht, in one of Germany's armed forces, but I had never heard about anyone in the family being a member of the Nazi party. I read the description again. Sturmabteilung. Stormtroopers. The SA. The paramilitary organization whose members served as Hitler's henchmen and helped bring the National socialist German Worker's Party into prominence.

I glance at the belt on my desk again. Now the fine hairs on my arms prickle. My stomach clenches.

I tap Hitler SA on the keyboard.

Founded in 1921 by an aspiring Hitler, most of the SA included WWI ex-soldiers and right-wing nationalists called the Freikorps. Angry and dissatisfied over the treatment of Germany under the

Treaty of Versailles, they were attracted to Nazi doctrine and the Austrian's enticing promise to make Germany great again. They first intimidated, then initiated violence against Communists and Jews, and disrupted meetings of Hitler's political opponents. They stood guard during Hitler's public speeches, a ready show of force. Called Brownshirts because of the color uniforms they wore, they fashioned themselves after Mussolini's Fascist Blackshirts. In 1931, Hitler named himself Supreme Leader of the SA. Ernest Rohm, a close confidante and Nazi party member, became Chief of Staff.

As I read about the SA, what strikes me most is the tendency towards violence. Political support, even quiet intimidation, I would expect, but as I read, I envision burly thugs with big chips on their shoulders, looking for trouble.

By 1933, Rohm and Hitler clashed in purpose and ideals of the National Socialist German Workers' Party. Rohm wanted to stress its socialistic side while Hitler focused on the nationalistic part. Rohm claimed that Hitler's rise to power would not have occurred without the loyalty of the lower- and middle-class Stormtroopers. He insisted that a second revolution needed to occur to purge the government of its remaining elite. Hitler focused on a superior society, and believed the true Aryans descended from elite classes. He disagreed with the need for a second revolution and insisted what the country needed most was economic stability and national pride.

In doing my research, I wondered about the name, National Socialist German Worker's Party, and learned that it had been an attempt to incorporate the two issues prevalent at the time. Nationalist and German appealed to identity and national pride, both of which had taken a big hit from WWI. Socialist and Workers was intended to attract working class people, necessary for votes, although it was not long before the truth of Hitler's vision came to light. Manipulation by semantics and lies. Himmler also had Hitler's ear in 1933, promoting purity of race.

By 1934, Rohm had built the SA to two million members and suggested that the army, the Reichswehr, could be integrated and become subordinate to the SA. Rohm, of course, would be put in charge. Senior military officers objected. Hitler was also aware of Rohm's open criticism: "Adolph is a swine. He will give us all away. He only associates with reactionaries now … Are we revolutionaries, or aren't we? We've got to produce something new … a new discipline. A new principle of organization. The generals are a lot of old fogies."

Dissension within organizations, especially political ones, never ends well.

Hitler promised to get rid of Rohm if the military generals would swear loyalty to him. They agreed. On June 30th, 1934, the Night of the Long Knives began, and by July 2nd, the entire leadership of the SA had been purged. In 1935, it was reorganized.

Math puts my great-uncle Johann, Oma's brother, into the proper time frame. Born in 1913, he was eighteen in 1931. Shortly after, his sister Katharina, one year older, was freshly married to Felix and lived in Deggendorf, a short distance away. In a few years she would have three young children and an absent husband. It was during this time she became pregnant with Sieglinde. If Johann had indeed joined the SA, or even just considered it, he would have been in the company of the men, and women, who participated in the Lebensborn program.

As I prepare for the next trip to Germany, I decide the time has come to 'fess up to taking the belt. I do not take it with me for fear it may be apprehended as contraband at the airport, either coming or going. But I do take a photo and plan to show it to my aunt. Sieglinde may have heard something about her uncle's involvement in the SA. Or she may tell me it didn't belong to him at all. With all things

The belt with SA symbol

related to the war, my family prefers to change the subject. I can't say I blame them. Many choices at the time were made for them, not by them. But whoever this belt belonged to made a conscious decision. Who? And why?

The Lies of Silence

The Tower
Sulzbach
June 2018

The red Mini-Cooper rental snakes through narrow streets, Tom-Tom navigation system confident of its route: *in 200 meters, turn right and you will have arrived at your destination.* The street dead-ends at the city wall which encases the Tower, my home for a week. I ease stiff legs onto the pavement after the three-hour drive from cousin Michael's house, pop the hatch, pull out a large suitcase, lug it up three steps and place it next to a small iron gate, then head back for the smaller one.

Behind me a car pulls up. I prepare a welcoming smile and walk out to meet Gabi Renner. I don't know her. She is the wife of recently deceased Erich Renner, the youngest son of great-uncle Johann. We had planned to meet last October, but I never made it, due to the injuries I sustained on that ill-fated trip. We've been emailing and I have a preconception of a kind, energetic woman. Gabi has been grief-stricken since Erich died after falling ill on vacation last summer. His death was not a shock; he suffered from auto-immune illnesses most of his life. *We knew he would not live into old age.*

Gabi steps out of her VW, head lifted with an expectant smile. I take a chance and throw arms around her for a hug, which she warmly returns. Petite and fit, her deep-set blue eyes sparkle in an alert face framed by short, windblown brown hair. I immediately like her. When she laughs, which she will do frequently, she chuffs a bit through her nose. While I dig my purse out of the front seat, she grabs the two suitcases and hauls them effortlessly up the ten steep steps to the landing and into the front room. I'm impressed.

A crack has caused a portion of the Tower's old stucco on the front to peel in a large swath. It gives the front entrance a bit of charm, aided by the ivy that crawls up and over the doorframe. Tiny bees hum as they hover over the sweet-smelling tiny white blooms. The old iron key creaks inside the lock, and the first door opens onto a small landing that contains a coat rack and a mat for muddy shoes. A second door opens into the kitchen and gathering area.

Once inside, I breathe deeply with anticipation of being in my beloved Tower for the next week. The walls seep the smells accumulated over hundreds of years. The furnishings have been replaced. The appliances are modern. It smells exactly as I expected, as it was for the child enamored with this fairy tale place.

Gabi and I sit at the wood-block kitchen table, recounting our family connection, and Erich's illness. We talk about her adult children; all three live out of town but nearby. Gabi beams when she speaks of them. I tell her how much the Tower means to me from my childhood. She assures me it will stay in our family as per the original documents. Her sons also have a deep love for it, as did her husband.

"Oh, it needs work. Especially the old roof. Sometimes when it rains, I climb into the attic, stand in the middle of the room and turn slowly around, looking for any drips. When I find one, I dig through a pile of broken adobe tiles piled up in the corner, look for the right size and shove it into the offending spot." She laughs. "It seems to work, although sometimes I need a few."

Can it be? The same pile of broken shards where I found the belt?

Taking a deep breath, I open my phone to scroll through photos, find the one I'm looking for and gently place it in front of Gabi. Her eyes widen.

I tell her about my visit here in 1983, and my foray into the attic. "This is what I found." I point to the photo.

Gabi's face does not register surprise. Instead, she chuffs a quick embarrassed laugh, a dismissive flutter of hands as her body leans away from the offending image. I babble on about my embarrassment at taking it, and admit that I have had it hidden all these years.

"Am I right in assuming it belonged to your husband's father?"

Her eyes dart around before they settle again on the photo.

"Yes. Possibly. Probably. This was a problem within the family."

After his father died, Erich found a photo album tucked away under personal items. In it was the proof that he never should have seen. Photos of his father's Nazi activities. Gabi does not elaborate. She goes quiet, as if the images are popping up in her mind.

"It was devastating for Erich. He adored his father. To think his father may have been a member of the Nazi Party, well, it was a hardship for him to deal with."

I ask her if it would be possible for me to look at the album while I am here. She nods slowly. A tiny sledgehammer is now thumping into the space between my eyes. I sense it's time for both of us to ponder this alone. The long drive down from Neustadt is beginning to take its toll. I also feel guilty for this impetuous decision to blindside Gabi with the photo of the belt. I ask her if we can spend time together again soon. She asks when? What are my plans for my stay?

I tell her I want to check in with Aunt Sieglinde who is leaving in a few days to go on retreat, and I will let her know. Gabi and I hug goodbye. As she drives away, I call my aunt who lives uptown from the Tower.

"Hallo Madlen!" Sieglinde chirps loudly through my phone. "I'm coming down. I'm so glad you're here!"

Ten minutes later I hear the front gate squeak and see her long legs appear at the open door. She holds out a tiny ruby red Kalanchoe plant, her lovely face lit up. We hug and laugh, glad to see one another. She sits in the kitchen chair vacated less than half an hour ago and I tell her about meeting Gabi, how I immediately liked her. Sieglinde nods and looks thoughtful.

"I don't know Gabi well. My uncle Johann died when he was only fifty-nine. He had congestive heart failure, maybe caused by diphtheria he suffered when young. Erich was the younger of his two boys. He and Gabi kept to themselves. Our families didn't get together for holidays or even stay in touch. After Johann's wife Kuni went into assisted living, I visited her regularly and prayed with her until she passed. It's sad that Erich is now gone. But Gabi has her family in town and her kids live close by. How is she doing?"

I tell her Gabi stays close to her children now and seems content. I also tell her that Gabi and I have plans to get together soon. But I decide not to mention our conversation about the belt. At least for now. We sit and catch up; laughter bubbles out of my ever-effusive aunt. She tells me she will be seeing her friend Martin, whom she met through church. He lives in a small town in what was once East Germany, several hours away. He's a widower and lives close to his children. But they make it a point of seeing each other several times a month. Sieglinde sighs and tells me how she misses her deceased husband, Schorsh, but that she also feels fortunate she has a companion for this time in her life. A spark to highlight her very golden years. And, of course, because she met him through the church, God approves.

Sieglinde's joy for the everyday is apparent in everything she says and does. And always after prayer and what she feels is her first and true Father's wishes for her. Just a little, I envy her certainty and peace of mind. How simple it would be to get up in the morning, ask what is expected of me that day, and receive an answer.

After she leaves, I text Gabi and tell her I'm free Monday. A few minutes later she responds. *I'll pick you up in the afternoon and bring you to my house. I have a stack of interesting old photos and documents we can sift through.*

Thoughts turn back to great-uncle Johann and the belt.

By the time he was in his teens, the National Socialist German Workers Party was gaining momentum. Hitler had recently been released from a year in prison after his attempted takeover of the

German government with the failed Beer Hall Putsch. The *Hitler Jugend,* Hitler Youth, became an official political organization in 1922. In 1929 the HJ was declared the only official youth group of the Nazi party for boys. The focus: athleticism, camaraderie, loyalty, and pride for country. Essentially, a good thing, right?

By the end of 1933, the membership was well over two million. By 1936, membership became mandatory and jumped to eight million. By 1939 stringent laws forced all boys aged ten and up to be a member. Every Saturday was devoted to HJ work. There were weekend camps, summer camps, training camps. The motto was, We are born to die for Germany. And the anthem: Now let the flags fly in the great dawn, which will light our way to new victories, or burn us to death.

Hitler was building his armed forces. He once stated: "He alone who owns the youth gains the future." The Hitler Youth organization would have provided an easy transition into the SA.

So it could have been for Oma's brother Johann.

•

On Monday Gabi picks me up late afternoon. When we get to her spacious home, Max the Spitz greets us with loud happy barks. He circles around me and sniffs my feet. Tiny pointed ears and black button nose quiver. After a brief tour of the flat, we settle in at her long white kitchen table. Gabi grabs an intimidating stack of musty paperwork from the kitchen counter and plops it in front of us. I take a deep breath, and we look at each other. She reminds me with a grin that she forewarned me.

Smiles fade when the first thing she opens is the leather-bound photo album that once belonged to Johann—the one with the incriminating black and white photos pasted onto thick black paper—that caused Erich so much grief.

Bavaria played an integral role in the rise of the Nazi Party. Nurnberg, about thirty-one miles west of Sulzbach-Rosenberg, is home to Hitler's ambitious project known as the *Reichsparteitagsgelände,* or the Rally Grounds. Monumental buildings for gatherings and marches cover about four square miles. Construction began in 1933 after Hitler's election as Chancellor. A street called the Great Road, one and half miles long and one hundred and thirty-two feet wide, served as a parade venue. Beginning in that year, six massive rallies had taken place by the time WWII began in September of 1939.

Johann would have been in his twenties. Pages of photos in that album are clearly of the rally grounds, which Gabi and I later visit. Imposing lines of uniformed men, arms raised in the Sieg Heil salute, march on the Great Road. Massive banners display the Hakenkreuz as it boldly lays claim to all. Gabi tells me that all German schoolchildren in Bavaria are now required to visit the complex, which includes the Documentation Center. A museum with a permanent exhibition titled Fascination and Terror contains life-size photo cutouts of Hitler, his henchmen, and scenes from concentration camps displayed in eerie lighting. It is a somber, frightening experience, meant as a warning.

Other photos in the album are of fit young men in various athletic activities, often dressed only in simple cotton shorts. They look like they are in their late teens or early twenties. We stare at the history depicted here. I take pictures with my cell phone, but we don't linger; we've seen enough. The next few hours are spent going through old and faded documents pertaining to the sale of the Tower and the renovations to make it more livable.

An interesting find in the stack of documents Gabi and I went through is a document dated December 14th, 1912, which passes ownership of the Tower to my great-grandparents from Martin's mother Barbara. His father had already died. Widow Renner was a wise woman, or perhaps one that had wise council. Page after page, line after line, old-fashioned script lays out her living conditions moving forward, including food and spending money. A few examples:

1.) Yearly: 1 Zentner (about 50 Kg) grain, 1/2 Zentner wheat, 1 Kg bovine lard, 20 fresh chicken eggs, and 3 Zentner nice-looking potatoes.

10kg pork, 15 sausages of different variety and a pound of Pressack *(a type of sausage); all this if you are butchering or not.*

Sauerkraut, as much as needed if available.

2.) Daily: 1/2 liter of good, sweet freshly milked milk as long as the cow of the estate still gives milk.

In general:

In case of sickness, the widow Barbara Renner will receive care at no cost to her; the costs of the doctor and the pharmacy will be borne by the inheritor.

The widow Renner will have space in the basement for storage, the right to use the kitchen and a place outside to store her wood. Should she be forced to move, she will receive thirty marks a year for expenses, and all the aforementioned items will be provided at a value of approximately one hundred marks. The inheritor will make certain his mother's living quarters and her clothes are clean. She will receive two bales of rye straw yearly for her bed mattress.

Wow. There is more, but we get the idea. Every need was listed. In 1912, at the writing of these stipulations, she was sixty-five. She lived another twenty years. Well cared for, it seems.

Nothing else pops up that can shed light on Johann's possible Nazi involvement.

•

Weeks later, back home in Florida, I scroll through the pictures I took. One photo of three young men I dismiss as another show of athleticism, until I notice something off on the edges, and zoom in. What I see almost makes me drop the phone.

It isn't horseplay at all. Instead, it depicts a youth forced onto grassy ground, on all fours. Dark forest looms in the background. Another man stands behind him, his left hand wrapped around a chunk of the victim's hair which pulls his face up at an odd angle. The aggressor clutches what may be a small knife in his right hand. Another man faces them, rippled abs straining above cotton shorts. His look is fierce. His fist is aimed at the face of the one on all fours. The victim's dark hair is long on top, part of it flops onto his face. The two aggressors have extremely short hair. In the HJ, boys who didn't meet certain criteria were teased, bullied, and beaten to get into line. It's the flip side of the camaraderie, and one that could have been a wakeup call for Johann. I look closely at the young men depicted in the photo, but none of them look like my great-uncle.

The expression on the victim's face is impossible to define. Superimposed on the entire photo is another one: ghosts of fresh-faced young women sitting in a circle on couches or chairs, relaxed and chatting, rim the edges. One girl's smiling face sits directly on the image of the victim's face. It's difficult to make out unless one zooms in dramatically. Looking at the photo with a naked eye one sees a blurriness. A creepy error in photo development turned into a horrific contrast of hate and innocence.

The question is: where did the photo come from? Did Johann take it? Or could I be mistaken and he's actually in the photo? If so, which one is he? When I ask Gabi she is unsure. We don't know if Johann took all the photos in the album. And if so, what was his reason for documenting this scene? Who are the girls in the superimposed photo? More questions we will probably never have the answers to.

As a young man with no family yet, the initial intrigue to join an elite group such as the SA was likely appealing. I prefer to think his moral upbringing eventually kicked him into sensibility—perhaps he witnessed more than just horseplay and decided to return home to work at the steel mill instead of joining the SA. There is no one left to ask what happened. And who would have known the details? My mother never mentioned anything. Just as Oma had been able to keep portions of her life out of afternoon kaffeeklatsch conversations, this too would have been a secret to tuck away, to pretend it never happened.

Shame has such power.

When I questioned Sieglinde about Johann's Nazi involvement over lunch one afternoon, she looked nonplussed for a few beats. Her knowledge would be limited to what she overheard as a child. She and her sister Christel spent summers at the Tower with their grandparents. When school finished in Montabaur in mid-June, Katharina would pack each one a small suitcase filled with freshly washed and ironed cotton dresses, pinafores, Mary Janes, and a pair of sturdy hiking boots, along with hair ribbons and soft flannel pajamas (the Tower tended to stay chilly, even in summer, from the thick stone walls). On sturdy pieces of paper, she wrote each girl's name, their home address and the address of the Tower, punched a hole on each side, threaded through a sturdy piece of twine and hung it around their respective necks. Then she made sure they were settled on the train. Their tickets were handed to the conductor along with instructions of where they needed to get off.

This would have been after the war ended. Johann was working as a locomotive engineer for Maxhütte, the large steel mill in the adjacent town of Rosenberg. He was in his early thirties, married, and lived nearby. When the girls tired of collecting pebbles out of the small stream that flowed behind the Tower or chasing the flock of chickens that lived in the courtyard, they could clasp hands and hike up the hill to their uncle's flat. A photo shows him in the traditional Bavarian lederhosen, sturdy shorts made of leather and held up by suspenders (typically worn for hard physical labor because they held up better than cotton or wool). Sieglinde smiled when I showed it to her.

"My Uncle Johann was very dear to me. He was a kind, loving person with warm eyes. I was always happy to see my uncle; he made me laugh and feel good. It's hard to imagine him involved in anything violent, much less the SA." She shrugged, palms up in apology. Sighed.

My aunt looked intensely into my eyes. "Those times are hard to understand now. I was a child, so it was what it was."

Hazing, backstory unknown.

Maxhütte Lost

The Tower
Sulzbach-Rosenberg
June 2018

Sieglinde opens the front door and comes in laughing. Shakes off raindrops after her dash from the car and up the steep steps into the Tower. I have coffee ready, and we settle ourselves at the kitchen table. I've just taken a shower to warm up. My bike ride this morning ended in a sprint back to the Tower during a drenching rainstorm.

I called Sieglinde when I got back to tell her where I'd been, at Maxhutte, the old steel mill where Martin worked most of his life. In the old photo album I have, there are many photos of him at the mill. Some were taken with his workers; in others he is with a group of management personnel in suits and hats. I've known that ironworks was a major industry for the area, but it wasn't until I accidentally ended up there today that I realized how massive and impressive it must have been. I found it because I got lost. I tell Sieglinde the whole story. She nods and says *ah ha* a lot.

•

The fickle sky is blue and clear when I start out from the Tower and get on a main road in a direction I hadn't taken before. After pedaling for two hours, I turn into a stretch of woods and come back out on a main road to go home. Except nothing looks familiar. A suited gentleman stands at a bus stop. I skid up to him and say, "Richtung Sulzbach, bitte," (directions to Sulzbach, please) and he nods, turns, and points in the opposite direction of where I'm headed. "Straight that way," he tells me. "For many kilometers". And grins. Really.

OK. I'm not surprised; I have a notoriously bad sense of direction. A smile, a wave, and I hop back on the bike. Now I look up and see angry clouds rolling in from over the mountains. In the near distance I see the looming concrete and steel buildings of Maxhutte and realize this is the Rosenberg section of Sulzbach-Rosenberg. The towns were separate municipalities in the Oberpfalz region until 1934, when they became one. Now that I'm here, I want to drive into the monolith industrial site that provided work for my maternal family and thousands more. There's got to be a place to hunker down and wait out the impending storm. I detour towards it.

The street and sidewalks are empty of civilization, although functional office buildings sit opposite the deserted plant. There is an eerie presence in the barrenness. I pause, senses on high alert. Perhaps I'm tapping into the long-gone ghosts of thousands of workers. Uropa Martin worked here in several capacities, beginning as a blast-furnace operator and ending up in management. Johann was a locomotive engineer for many years. Whereas Sulzbach had an impressive history dating back to the early eighth century with its castle and succession of dukes and counts, Rosenberg was a vital industrial center.

Since the Middle Ages, rich iron deposits were mined along a swath of 120 kilometers that began in upper Franconia and ran south through Bavaria to Regensburg. The Bavarian Iron Route is part of the Cultural Path of Iron, a network that continues through Austria, Poland, Slovenia, Hungary, Romania, and Italy. And what was all this iron used for in the Middle Ages, you might ask? Well, think agricultural tools like pitchforks, rakes, shovels, and so forth. But also think weaponry, like cannons and cannonballs, and armor for gallant knights. Let's not forget the essential torture chamber ensemble that included thumbscrews, foot screws, branding irons and the notorious Iron Maiden, a casket-like device with spikes used to impale its victims alive. Iron created wealth, built castles, and provided work for thousands.

Steel production began at the new MaximiliansHütte, (named after Bavarian King Maximilian II) in 1853 (coincidentally, the same year Leonhard Renner purchased the Tower) and grew into a massive facility that eventually employed almost 10,000 people. Five massive blast furnaces burned day and night. After a peak in the 1960s, the demand for steel dropped. In April of 1987, the first bankruptcy occurred. Work continued to dwindle, and in 1998 the second bankruptcy followed. By 2002, the remaining 450 employees clocked out for the last time. Labor protests made national news. The local unemployment office was filled with desolate and angry men.

Now the buildings sit and brood over a lost dynasty. Impressive and semi-intact, Maxhutte serves as a technical monument; it was the only plant in Europe that covered all stages of ore production in a confined space. The town museum devotes an entire floor to it. Most impressive is a display of a blast furnace, a scene straight out of Dante's Hades, fed day and night by hooded creatures. Silica, raw iron ore, coke, and limestone were dumped into a massive steel stack lined with refractory brick, while preheated air was blown from the bottom. As the materials descended, pure iron was separated and became liquid slag. Once activated, a blast furnace could run continuously for years.

As imposing, and now depressing, as the complex is, it is a testament to accomplishment. Thousands of folks gladly traded their beautiful countryside for a steady income. The hard labor and sooty skies were a way of life accepted without personal stigma. I think again about the belt, and the lure of joining the elite Nazi paramilitary unit for great-uncle Johann. The promise of something more. Yes, I can try to understand. Especially when I look at photos: his confident stance, his proud face.

Dark, dirty, industrial, abandoned. During WWII, the work here must have been frenetic. I can almost hear the pounding of machinery and men shouting, see massive billows of smoke spew out of multiple chimneys, smell steam hissing from the locomotive as it idles. I envision gaunt, strained faces of too-thin men, some with gloves and many without, grunting as they overload open box cars. Black soot drifts down like snow from hell. Are these the ghosts I felt as I sat in the street straddling my bike? How fitting, then, that the thunder boomed and the lightning sparked and the heavens wept.

•

I ask my aunt if Sulzbach was dirty then. She says Rosenberg was, but the winds tended to favor Sulzbach, and she doesn't recall it as sooty. It's almost impossible to imagine a bustling town filled with thousands working and living amidst noisy blast furnaces and gray soot plumes in this now idyllic landscape. And where did everyone live, piled on top of one another in tiny flats? How much additional industry—shops and restaurants—existed and faded away along with the plant? There are no deserted buildings. The land is green and lush with nature.

Sulzbach had also been vital. In 1353, the town served as the capital of the New Bohemia after Count Palatine Rudolf II pledged the city to Emperor Karl IV, the ruler of Bohemia (now the Czech Republic). This was the first attempt to establish a modern state in a medieval realm and it was a success. Authorization to mine ore was granted. The city expanded and prospered. A succession of dukes and counts from different houses followed along through the centuries until the last duke of Palatinate-Sulzbach abolished the government in Sulzbach in 1791.

Sieglinde and I sip our coffee and look out onto the main castle wall.

"The town needed money desperately in the first part of the last century, so they started selling the empty castle buildings and any part of the wall thick enough to slap up a building. It was also during this time that the Tower came up for sale. About the same time, the steel mill started up and our descendants, who were farmers, moved into town for work." Sieglinde tells me.

I mention Johann and how the lure of something more, such as the status of the Nazi Party, may have been appealing to him. Sieglinde nods and shakes her head simultaneously.

"*Na ja*, it could be. I was so little then and afterwards no one spoke about the war. I do remember hearing that even Opa Martin considered joining the Nazis. But he was settled in at the steel mill, overseeing the forced labor that was brought in from other countries. *Ach*, who knows? I think many men at least considered joining. To have that power and status in town! But also many people were afraid and kept their heads down, waiting for the war to be over. Waiting to have plenty of food again."

Maxhutte Steel Mill, circa 1960.

Hunger and Poverty

The Tower
Sulzbach
June 2018

Sieglinde yells up the steps at the open front door of the Tower.

"Hurry, put your shoes on and come. Quickly! I left our lunch cooking on the stove. What a useless phone you have. I've been texting and trying to call, with no connection."

And in she comes, leaving her Skoda SUV idling by the front gate. I grab my bag and run out, flustered. When we get in the car, I check my phone. Nothing. Hmmm.

We wind uphill on the narrow cobblestone streets. Three minutes later we park in front of her large townhouse. Up the stairs we gallop, just in time. Veggies in a large pan have turned darkly crisp. Sieglinde is jabbering about my crappy phone again. When we sit down to a sautéed casserole of root vegetables, I ask to look at hers. I see the problem.

"Tante Sieglinde, you forgot to push send. See, it's still sitting here." I point.

She spits out laughter, along with a tiny chunk of turnip. Shrugs and rolls her eyes at herself.

Our food is delicious. While I'm staying at the Tower, we have fallen into the habit of eating lunch together, a comfortable companionship in her cozy kitchen. Yesterday I stopped at the fish market and bought a beautiful cut of fresh salmon. Sieglinde sautéed it in olive oil with a touch of sea salt and dill and served it alongside a medley of vegetables from her garden and a big salad. Her kitchen is a long and narrow room, separated from the rest of the house. A large casement window opens onto the cobblestone street below, which is filled with retail shops.

I remember sitting here as a child one afternoon and hearing the church bells from the Lutheran cathedral on the corner begin to chime. I hung out of the window and saw a wedding party leaving the sanctuary. Knowing it was customary for the bride to toss coins into the street for children to chase, I flew out of the kitchen and down the stairs to join in. It wasn't long before I slunk back to the kitchen, head down, clutching not a single coin. I remember stamping my feet, angry and disappointed, more so when I was chastised for my emotional display.

Sieglinde keeps a magnificent garden a few kilometers away at the edge of town. It's typical for folks to lease garden space away from their homes. Called *Schrebergärten,* these garden colonies are situated in rows and typically include a grill and picnic spot, along with a small hut or *schuppen.* The founder of this gardening concept, Dr. Daniel Schreber from the large and crowded city of Leipzig, first came up with the idea for safe outdoor spaces for city children to play in. When WWI started, these plots became valuable for growing food. What began as a breath of fresh air in smog-filled areas of the 1800s industrial revolution is now a must have for many German city-dwellers. It's estimated that over a million plots exist. They tend to measure just under an acre, separated by fencing, gate, and key.

Sieglinde's plot has a koi pond, a gnarly pear tree, and several ancient apple trees, branches furry with moss. Her rustic cabin is fully equipped with a kitchen, bathroom, and wood stove. Bunk beds sleep six. Last year the pear tree yielded bushels of fruit, most of which she pressed into juice. This year, her apple trees are struggling due to a premature warming period that caused the trees to blossom early. A return frost killed most of the delicate blooms; a few small green apples are hanging on. Sieglinde walks around the tree, *tsking*. Stops to cradle a small green survivor and mutters at it to hang in there until September. Lifts her eyes to the sky and says a small prayer.

Neat rows of turnips, onions, potatoes, yellow squash, and lettuces require daily care during season. A few days ago, we stripped her *Johannisbeeren* bushes clean. The juicy red currants, which remind me of lingonberries, are tart-sweet and commonly made into pies. When I thought I was done, having plucked all but the smallest berries, Sieglinde came behind me and finished it off. I think about this now as she swipes her empty plate with her index finger and joyfully licks it clean. I see her eyeball my plate.

One morning, when we were at Thomas' house together, I got up to clear the breakfast table, having eaten all but a few spoonfuls of muesli. Sieglinde snatched my bowl with a shocked expression.

"I grew up in the war. We can never, ever waste food."

She must have taught Thomas well, since he too finishes whatever I leave behind. Even in restaurants.

My aunt and her sisters spent much of their childhood either gathering food or wishing for more. She told me a story of exchanging a beloved doll for sugar. Curiously, Mom once told Jackie this same story, except that it was *her* doll. I suppose it could have happened twice. Or the event for one was so traumatic that both remembered it vividly. When I was growing up, Mom used to hoard certain foods, most notably butter and anything sweet. She once gave me a package of Christmas Lebkuchen, that delectable gingerbread confection. Excited, I bit into a cookie only to gag and spit. When I checked the packaging, I saw it had expired two years before.

For Sieglinde, anything edible is inherently gold. One afternoon her son Markus brought us zip-lock bags of deep-red Goji berries, touted as a superfood and priced accordingly. While I was nibbling out of my bag, I dropped one of the tiny, dried berries. Since we were engaged in conversation, I glanced at it and planned to pick it up later. Sieglinde snatched it up and popped it into her mouth. A second later the look on her face told me she had just realized her action. She looked at me and shrugged; it had been pure reflex.

I tend to eat small portions. This means there is almost always food left on my plate. Papa, at a recent lunch outing, shook his head sadly while staring at my half-finished meal, and expounded on my childhood habits with food. He said he "had watched me push valuable nutrition around on my plate," while grousing and scowling. He pointed a finger at me and said a serious discussion had taken place about my non-eating habits. I'm not sure if that meant my behind got swatted or if he actually tried to reason with me. His lessons didn't stick. I remained a skinny, picky eater for most of my youth.

For a moment right now, think about *those times*, and being relentlessly hungry during the war. There is not enough of anything, because all commodities are directed toward the war effort, especially food. Family rations were continually cut as the war raged on and Herr Hitler needed anything edible for his starving troops. At least in the country, in small farm towns such as Montabaur, vegetables and fruits were still grown and harvested. Like my grandmother, most families had small gardens and perhaps a few chickens. The shortages were more prominent in the larger cities that depended on transport and distribution.

By 1944, Germany was a bombed-out hull, with no way to transport food from the farms that were still able to produce. The Allies were pushing through the German countryside. They commandeered farms for shelter and food. Families would wrap up hams, eggs, and any other valuables, and tuck them deep into their manure piles. Once this was discovered, the first thing Allied soldiers did was grab pitchforks and start flinging shit. It's also how Father survived as a POW: able-bodied men were used as forced labor at farms to grow badly needed crops.

When I questioned my aunts about lack of food, both Sieglinde and Christel shrugged, and said, "Well, we managed to get enough to stay alive, right?" As children, they would pile on the family bicycle, one girl on the back, the other on the handlebars. With Katharina pedaling, they sneaked into the fields after harvest to pick through the dirt for anything left behind. The main shortage was in foodstuffs that couldn't be grown, such as sugar.

"I went with Mutti to get the ration book. We would then pick up our necessities, but Mutti would also buy a bar of dark bitter chocolate. Each of us children got one square. It was so exciting!" Sieglinde's eyes shone when she told me.

No wonder the doll story is so well remembered; it too was bittersweet.

Our brain alone needs 500 calories of glucose to function properly. The remainder of our caloric intake goes to our bodies. Since children's bodies are growing and developing, a lack of nutrition can cause irreparable damage. Studies done by Harvard Medical School on seventy-seven children hospitalized for severe starvation syndrome at an average age of seven months showed negative and long-lasting personality traits. Once they were in a high-nutrition program and physically caught up with normal growth curves, they still tended toward moodiness, anxiety, fear, depression, and anger, along with discomfort in social settings.

I can't help but think of my mother when I read about these traits. Without confirmation, I can't assume that poor nutrition was a contributing factor to Mom's personality. But she certainly lacked the ability to be harmonious. She also had ulcers. By middle age, more than half her stomach had been surgically removed. We now know ulcers are typically caused by H. Pylori bacteria, or by large doses of aspirin, which my mother swallowed daily for her arthritis. But for years, Mom's condition was blamed on anxiety and a tendency to stomach bile. Throughout the day, she nibbled on sweets and drank coffee, while a thin ribbon of smoke drifted towards the ceiling from a lit cigarette in an ashtray nearby.

What has been mentioned numerous times by my aunts and my mother is the extreme poverty they endured after Felix left. By the time she was thirty-six, Oma needed to provide for a family of seven, so she cleaned offices, mended clothes, and rented out the spare attic room. The children's clothes were always hand-me-downs. Family linens were carefully mended and used over and over. Every *Pfennig* was counted and treasured.

As a child, Christel helped clean offices, and her Mutti gave her a shiny Pfennig. She kept these in a ceramic container, on her nightstand. When she collected ten, she would go to the store and trade them in for a ten-cent piece. Her cache slowly grew. One day, she found her container empty. As she stormed around the house asking what had happened to her treasure, she came upon her brother Hans Herbert gobbling nuts and candy out of a store bag. Christel says she never forgave him.

After I was born and went to live with Oma, the stipend that Mom sent regularly provided a few breaths of relief. Our large garden yielded fresh produce. Occasionally there was pot roast or a baked chicken on Sundays. Rickety wooden shelves in our cellar were filled with preserved foods to tide us through winter.

Once I turned five, I could traipse up the hill to buy fresh rolls at the *Bäckerei* which I tucked into my pinafore to carry home. A local dairy farmer dropped off milk and butter, and neighborhood chickens contributed plenty of eggs. Lunch was a warm meal and could be a casserole, or soup with vegetables and some type of noodles. Pickled cabbage took the form of sauerkraut or braised red cabbage. Potatoes were a staple. Heavy, dense bread was served with cold cuts for *Abendessen*, our evening meal.

Some days, around four in the afternoon, the world for me became magical as neighbors came by for afternoon coffee. Oma would pull a crisp white tablecloth with lace edges out of the mahogany buffet. Snap, snap, and a flip onto the dining table as her red, gnarled hands smoothed it to perfection. Creamy porcelain dessert plates and matching coffee cups with delicate curved handles were lifted out of the china cabinet and arranged on the table.

Then a magnificent torte was placed in the center: buttery layers of white cake cushioned with fresh fruit, or a chocolate cake with cherries and walnuts. But that wouldn't be all—oh no. Tiny tea cookies, sugary donuts with squishy raspberry filling, and crispy swirls of fried dough studded with almonds. At Yuletide, Pfeffernuss, thumb-size cookies infused with spices and coated with powdered sugar were served along with traditional lebkuchen. The dried fruit cake called stollen, my favorite, was gobbled up with a thick slab of fresh yellow butter. On days when we didn't have visitors, we still had our afternoon coffee. But then we would sit at our old Formica kitchen table and nibble on leftover pastries or bread. For me it was a spoonful of coffee with lots of fresh milk. Oma had hers strong and black with a touch of milk and a cigarette.

But this was in 1959. Quality of life was on the mend.

After the war ended in 1945, food continued to be scarce. The American Occupation Forces policy to refuse food aid to Germans was presumably fueled by the atrocities seen in the concentration and work camps. The Occupation Forces depended almost entirely on imported goods, but they were not shared with the German populace.

During the war, millions of forced laborers imported from occupied countries lived under deplorable conditions. Many starved. Ironically, it was the loss of these workers that contributed to a shortage of food after the war. Displaced people filled the roads on their way home, leaving a lack of workers on the farms and in production. Granaries and food production facilities had been destroyed by bombing, as well as railroads and other means of transport.

Adding to the food aid embargo, the winter of 1946, with temperatures as low as minus twenty-two Fahrenheit, lasted until March of 1947. Parts of the Rhine froze, hampering the transportation of goods. Germans refer to this time as Weisser Tod (White Death) and Schwarzer Hunger (Black Hunger). The average food intake of German citizens was estimated to average between 1,000 and 1,500 calories a day. Malnutrition and starvation continued to plague the German people, who were seen as the evil that supported Hitler, not as victims who may not have had a choice.

I imagine once again the knock on Oma's door late at night. A tall, uniformed man in the shadows hands her gifts of necessity: a chunk of ham, some eggs, coal for the stove. Maybe some coffee. Or sweets für die Kinder. In exchange for the unspoken duty to country. To the Führer.

Perhaps she simply did what she had to do.

See No Evil, Hear No Evil

Journal
Bad Nauheim
July 2018

The notes I scrambled to write today began with a disclaimer by my father: *Most of the German people did not know about the gas chambers.* I don't remember if I brought it up or if he did. What I have learned by now is what a principled man Papa is. As he said this, he shook his head, a troubled look on his face, eyes not meeting mine. It could have been guilt, it could have shame, but it was probably sorrow.

We were sitting in his office where his computer is set up with dual monitors to aid his poor eyesight. Papa can pull up a document on one, then zoom in dramatically on individual words on the other. This allows him to track where on the document he's reading. He also wears the magnifying goggles that make him look like a mad scientist or a close-up of a bug, eyes huge in his sharp-angled face. Painstaking to be sure. But for my father, essential. He worries about the day his macular-degenerated eyesight will be so poor nothing will aid it.

He keeps a German/English dictionary open whenever I come over. If I'm unable to understand a word in our conversation, he jumps up and looks for the translation in English. He had just looked up *Entschädigung*, or indemnification. I wondered if he was going to explain how Germany had attempted to deal with its collective guilt concerning the Jewish genocide.

He sat back with a sigh and looked up at the ceiling.

"After the war ended, the Allied soldiers took the townspeople through the camps, forced them to look at hell. When they showed pictures of Bergen Belsen—the skeletal prisoners barely hanging on to life, the gas chambers, or showers as they were called—mein Gott! People shouted 'Liars, this can't be real!' At the Allied soldiers. Others couldn't live with the knowledge. They became broken. Not able to live a normal life after knowing the truth."

From conversations with my aunts, I think this lack of awareness may have been possible for many small-town folks. People in the villages and towns that dotted the country may not have known the full extent of the genocide. Yet even the smallest towns had at least a smattering of Jewish families. Everyone in town became aware of the decrees that denied certain rights. The businesses that were closed or destroyed, the separation in schools and, eventually, the separation of living areas as the Jewish populace was herded into ghettos. Once they began to be transported to labor and concentration camps, the story was that they were sent to "work."

Fear kept those who watched, and did know, quiet.

My mother told Jackie that she witnessed an awful sight one afternoon as a child. As she was walking past a local Jewish-owned grocery store in Montabaur with one of her sisters, a military transport vehicle screeched up to the door of the shop and the Gestapo marched in. A few minutes later, a child was dragged out of the store by his hair and tossed into the back of a truck. This was repeated for the entire family, the shop was ransacked, and the truck roared off. Stunned, the girls hurried home to report what they had seen. And were told by Mutti to forget what they saw, to tell no one.

Especially in the last eighteen months of the war, the Nazi regime was desperate to quash any of the rumormongering as they called it—any talk of the Final Solution was punishable by imprisonment or worse. People, especially the elders, pressed their lips together and chose to express their shame through silence, rather than speak of *those horrors*. The Wehrmacht losses in the Russian territories and in Africa were also not discussed for fear of reprisal. Propaganda became ever more strident as the regime began to understand it was losing the war. Any German citizen who commented on or questioned its veracity could be swiftly punished.

Yet, Hitler was initially hailed as the man who brought Germany back from the devastation and reparations of WWI. He was called the savior of German pride. I remembered a story my mother had once told me. To the best of my recollection:

Hitler came through Montabaur one spring to inspect the new garrisons. It was close to his birthday. Beforehand, the mayor ordered all young girls to come to the Rathaus, our City Hall. He had us line up as he walked back and forth looking at us, sometimes cupping a face for closer inspection. He picked me. I was six years old. He told me I would be the one to hand Hitler a bouquet of roses and wish him a happy birthday. I felt proud. Mutti made me a new dress to wear. I curtsied when I handed Hitler his flowers.

A few weeks later, on April 20th, Hitler received a priceless gift for his forty-ninth birthday. The movie *Olympia* premiered to rave reviews, not only in Germany but worldwide. Leni Riefenstahl, who wrote, directed, and produced the film with Hitler's money, would win awards and embark on a grand global tour for her beautiful imagery of the 1936 Olympics. Its message was one of unity and peace. A year later, the world would discover it had been conned. *Olympia* is now seen as the clever piece of propaganda Hitler intended. He presented to the world a country strong and confident, filled with pride and unified under his leadership. He promised peace in return for acceptance.

A boycott almost didn't fail. Germany had been awarded the 1936 Olympics in 1931, while still under the leadership of General Paul von Hindenburg. But in April of 1933, a few months after Hitler became Chancellor, an Aryans only policy had been established in German sports organizations. Countries in Europe and America called for a boycott. It was narrowly overturned by the International Olympic Committee. As athletes flooded into Germany for the games, Hitler decreed that any signs reflecting anti-Semitism be taken down. As a token, he allowed Helene Mayer, who had won the gold medal for fencing at the 1932 Olympics in Amsterdam, to participate even though her father was Jewish. She went on to win a silver medal.

The hatred, ostracizing, and execution of the Jewish people was a gradual, as well as a historic, process. The underlying prejudice had simmered for many generations. Hitler initially used it to his advantage in gaining power before his ranting created the kind of virulent hatred that fed unimaginable violence. Other groups were targeted at the same time. Communists, Romani or what were known at the time as Gypsies, homosexuals, Afro-Germans, Jehovah's Witnesses, and anyone with disabilities were considered undesirable.

In reading about his life, there are no overt signs of anti-Semitism in Hitler's youth. The doctor who treated his beloved mother Klara as she lay dying of breast cancer was a Jewish man, Eduard Bloch. He tried everything to save her, including a radical treatment known as iodoform, an early type of chemotherapy. Hitler was only seventeen at the time. It has been said that his father was cold and distant. Her death was devastating.

Bloch was later quoted as saying "In all my career, I have never seen anyone so prostrate with grief as Hitler." And grateful to the doctor who tried valiantly to save her. In 1940, he encouraged and helped Bloch and his family's emigration to the United States.

I find that whenever I bring up the word (Jew, Jewish, Juden) to my relatives, the person I'm speaking to immediately looks down or away as they attempt to slide into another subject. My Germans are simple folk imbued with good character and morals. They are kind to each other, respect life in general, work hard and live honestly. Yet my grandmother, my mother and her siblings, my father and his family, all lived within the bubble of Nazi propaganda which turned into the silence of fear.

Jewish people were not the first to be gassed by the Nazi regime. From late 1939 to August of 1941, over 70,000 Germans were herded through the earliest gas chambers disguised as "showers." These were handicapped men, women, and children. Under a program called *T4 Aktion*, they were deemed *lebensunwert*, or life-unworthy. It took the bravery of a German Catholic Cardinal, Clemens August Graf von Galen to speak out against the evil of killing innocent people that resulted in a temporary abatement.

The program continued quietly with estimates of up to 300,000 killed by 1945. However, focus and history concentrate on the Jewish persecution and genocide. Printed and filmed propaganda permeated the German people's daily life to advance the premise that the Jewish Race was sub-human. *Untermensch*. This was usually accompanied with grossly distorted drawings of small evil eyes in a sharp face, eclipsed by a long bulbous or hooked nose.

•

Yesterday Papa and I rode a bus to Butzbach, about eleven kilometers northwest of Bad Nauheim. It's a beautiful old town filled with fachwerk houses, many dating back to the 1600s. Fachwerk load-bearing construction consists of massive vertical, diagonal and horizontal timber beams designed in a grid, then filled with plaster or clay. A rustic farmhouse façade. We walked around and settled on an Italian bistro for lunch. Next door was the town museum, which touted the traveling Anne Frank exhibition out of Berlin. Thrilled, I pointed to it and asked if we could go through.

Ja, natürlich.

Once inside the lobby, my attention was diverted by photos and literature depicting the American occupation in the 1960s. A town of about 12,000 residents, Butzbach was inundated with 10,000 plus troops housed just outside town limits. Imagine an influx of American military with its phalanx of jeeps and tanks. Barracks hastily thrown up. Soldiers filling the streets and restaurants, boisterous and loud. I learned about this from a no-nonsense docent at the museum, lips pursed with the importance of her information. She also showed us a newspaper article about a young woman raped and murdered by an American soldier. It was part of the display.

I stood silently and read. Father proudly informed the docent that I was his daughter from America. The elderly woman stared at me and shook her head sadly. She touched my arm and told me about how life changed in the town for many years, because of the Americans. A castle that had functioned as a German military installation in the nearby town of Kirch Gons, Schloss Kaserne, was also taken over by the Americans at the end of WWII. It became the largest military base in Europe for the Army Combat Brigade.

The docent pulled out a massive book a local author had written about the Butzbach occupation, filled with photos. One showed a seemingly unending line of railroad cars sitting at the train depot, filled with American tanks. The docent nodded grimly. "Yes, the cars stretched for five kilometers."

I noticed the date: 1981. I looked at her, puzzled. "So this was long after the initial occupation?"

"Oh, by now they were waiting for WWIII to begin with Russia. We had troops here for many years. Following the end of the Cold War in the early 1990s, over two hundred military bases were closed throughout Germany, including Butzbach," she added, looking relieved.

The Anne Frank exhibit was extensive. It included life-sized black and whites of Anne, her family and the hiding place that was their life for twenty-five months. As I wandered through, thoughts heavy, and heart aching, Papa patiently waited for me in the lobby. He sat on a bench. His head rested on the hand that held his walking stick between his knees, his face thoughtful.

•

Sulzbach, a week later

Sieglinde pulls up in her SUV on Sunday after church. Her middle son Markus is with her. Tall and earthy, he slings long arms around me in a bear hug. His boyhood freckles are gone, along with his shock of red hair, his pate bare and shiny like his brothers'. We stop for lunch and come out into a brilliant, relaxing mid-afternoon sun. Markus suggests a lake nearby, the Happurger See, as perfect for a digestive walk-around.

Happurger is a gorgeous reservoir that feeds a nearby power plant. It is deemed too small for power boats. Instead, a couple of sloops skim along on the fresh easterly breeze, joined by a smattering of paddle-boarders. A walking path encircles it and follows carefully planted shade trees. Families and couples stake claims to patches of grass. White skin gleams in the sunshine. Most folks have a dog or two who loll in the water, tongues hanging.

Sieglinde points to the mountain Houbirg, which is more like a tall hill. It is possible to see a flat site cleared of vegetation, and what appears to be an entrance of some kind. We are discussing what it might possibly be, when my ever-effusive aunt stops an elderly man, power-walking from the opposite direction, and asks if he knows.

Head bobbing, he tells us we are looking at the entrance of Doggerstollen, tunnels and rooms built inside the mountain. During WWII, long before the reservoir and bucolic countryside, there was a concentration camp called Hersbruck, named after the small town it was closest to. Prisoners hiked five kilometers daily from the camp up into the mountain to excavate an area planned for the use of manufacture and storage of BMW airplane parts. Statistics state at least thirty prisoners a day died during this undertaking; 4,000 out of 9,000 laborers perished. Two shifts worked back-to-back. It was a way to get hard work done, and for some, especially the Jews, the policy often was annihilation by work.

Excavation began in May 1944, but only 15,000 meters of a planned 100,000 were completed by April 1945 when the Allies filled towns and skies around Nurnberg. The project, code name *Ash 1*, was abandoned. More than 600 prisoners were marched toward Dachau in Munich, about 160 kilometers away. Exhausted and starving, many died along the way. Now the huge steel entrance doors remain closed and locked. There is talk of opening a portion of the tunnels as a memorial to those prisoners who died.

Sieglinde, who has lived in this area most of her life, is unaware of the existence of the project. Her face registers shock. Markus tries to keep a poker face, although he admits he also didn't know. But he probably wouldn't. Although his generation is all too aware of the historical discrepancies concocted for years to cover up the true horrors inflicted during Hitler's reign, this is not a subject discussed lightly, if at all.

For my maternal family, the Jewish were part of community life and town commerce. They were neighbors and friends. The town of Sulzbach now boasts as a landmark the Jewish Printing House which first opened in 1669. Under the Frankel-Arnstein family, it achieved renown throughout Europe. The local synagogue, rebuilt after a devastating city fire in 1822, was considered one of the most beautiful in Germany. Current town literature boasts *Jews were welcome in Sulzbach beginning in 1666. The entrance to what was once known as Germany's most beautiful synagogue attests to the many centuries of Jewish life in Sulzbach.* By 1933, the Jewish population stood at nine, down from 336 in 1881. Five of them emigrated. On January 21, 1943, the last one remaining was sent to a ghetto.

Exploited by the Nazis to rally the average populace into a sense of belonging, nationalism was presented as pride to the average German Volk for their heritage and country. History lessons in school have changed as Germany has taken accountability for the acts of a man who orated his sick visions into power. Who manipulated with remarkable canniness the average man, woman, and child to scream their allegiance under the guise of devotion to country and the German spirit. Until it was too late.

Outlander

Munich
July 2018

Yesterday I drove the death-defying autobahn from Sulzbach to visit Sieglinde's son Thomas and his family in Munich. I got in late and have now traipsed bleary-eyed into the cheerful kitchen late this morning to the smell of freshly ground coffee beans. Thomas is home, but his wife has gone off to work and the boys walked to school hours ago. I pour a mug and plop down at the table. After the usual concern about how I slept and how I feel, my cousin continues to stand and stare at me, mouth opening and closing as he organizes English words in his head.

"You are quite unusual. I think you live comfortably with two feet firmly hovering over two continents," he finally ventures.

Thomas the psychotherapist. I raise my left eyebrow at him. There's more he wants to tell me. And ask me.

"Well," he continues and pushes out his lower lip, cradling a mega-cup of coffee, long legs splayed, brow furrowed. "Your life began in Germany, with two German parents, then you were taken to America by your mother and new stepfather, and you … vanished. Since we talked a few years ago, you're back in our family, building relationships. I see you hovering with one foot planted above each country, straddling the ocean. It seems easy for you, to have two homes."

Oh, Thomas. Do you know the word *Zerrissenheit*?

There is a constant inner tugging that wears on me. The shift as my sister and brother became halves and Ted my step-father. Now I have a father, a step-mother and a half-brother that have taken precedence. I continue to yearn to be here—somewhere, anywhere—to be close to Papa so I can see him when it works for him. He has a life and doesn't have a hole to fill, but I believe it is a joy for him to go walking with me, to sit on a bench in one of the glorious parks or a coffeehouse to talk about his life and the things he wants to share with me. But I cannot live here.

•

I need time to gather wildly careening thoughts and corral them into submission. The time spent with my father and his family made me, once again, painfully aware of an outlander status, now in both my native country and my adopted one. I thought about a passage I read yesterday in *Field Guide for Getting Lost,* a Rebecca Solnit favorite. A chapter about captives in history and how they lost who they were to become someone else out of necessity. They reinvented themselves. Solnit phrased this reinvention as a psychological metamorphosis. I suppose this is what I also did; all those years of attempted reinvention. Could I conceivably change back?

I shuttle back and forth across the pond like I'm visiting relatives in the next town. I pretend nonchalance. But it's bullshit. The Germans have a marvelous word for my feelings: Zerrissenheit. It translates into torn-apart-ness. Disunity is more concise. And it comes at me in waves. I had been an accidental child, my grandmother's ward, German-bred, American-raised. A transplant desperate to ditch her German-ness in dogged pursuit of the chimera of American-ness.

I think again of the first two years of school. The lack of memories, with only class photos to prove I was there. I didn't look any goofier than my classmates—we all had bad haircuts that looked like they were done by our moms—but I felt like the class dweeb. None of the kids look especially mean, or too cool. After all, we're talking about first graders here. And we were all military brats, essentially nomads.

I chose to blame my ineptness on being German, which I learned from Mom's struggles to fit in. My stepfather had high visibility on Post. As did my very German mother, with her brusque accent. A brutally honest person, she refused to employ niceties while fluttering a delicate hand. The other officers' wives did more than shun her. They made her life miserable with false kindness that turned into snide rebukes. Not understanding the interplay of adults, I decided it was a blight to be German. Stuck my heritage into a file and drop-kicked it into the farthest alcoves of my mind.

Being an Army brat has its advantages when you want to try on new personas. We moved every year or two. Each time became a chance for a new beginning. I gathered the threads to weave a mantle of American-ness, only to pull out all the stitches to start over. There was the cool kid who flaunted rules; the aloof kid, too mysterious to have friends; the kind kid who attempted to befriend everyone; the tough kid who suffered from some unknown tragedy … whatever.

My tweens and teens were unending days of anxiety, every emotion heightened by uncertainty. Mom and I lived in constant strife with each other. She continued to have bouts of depression, for which my immature mind had no tolerance. I lashed out with insults. In turn, she tried to control me with criticism. Being at home only reinforced feelings of being unmoored. As I had done my entire life, when things unraveled in school, or with the friends I did have, I believed there was no safety net to catch me, no one to turn to.

In 1971 I turned sixteen. Ted retired from the Army and moved our family to St. Petersburg, on the west coast of Florida. I found a weekend job at the local Whataburger and took up with a group of neighborhood kids who were as aimless as I was. One of the boys became my best friend. When he quit school and moved to the Florida panhandle to work for his father's construction company, I thought I was in love and followed him. At eighteen we married. A bad decision as it turned out.

As the passion of married life fizzled out in my mid-twenties, I headed back to school and immersed myself in English literature.

Now I had a firm identity: student. And after, graduate student with a BA in English. A small patch of terra firma to navigate from. When Mom phoned in the spring of 1983 and asked me to accompany her and Jackie to Germany for a long-overdue visit, it was this patch of solid ground that gave me the confidence to agree. It was time to readdress the heritage I had spent years dismantling and shedding. I intended to be as American as possible. This meant I would compare the difference in everything, sure that I would find my Americanness superior.

Instead, I fell in love with my aunts, uncles, and cousins, along with their, and my, beautiful country, and wanted to return soon. But life got busy. I started a career in corporate sales which became a successful business venture. I married, gave birth to a son, and felt like I was settled at last. An American wife, entrepreneur, and mother.

In 2016 everything changed when I found my father.

The part of identity shrouded for an entire life now raised itself with a triumphant wagging finger. In the time my father and I have spent together, I've discovered how German I really am. How well my looks, habits and attitude fit. How comfortable I feel just being me, here in my homeland. The time I am spending with him, his family and my old family is a time of delicious ease. It is acceptance. Both ways: mine of just letting me be me, and theirs of enfolding me into the family. Accepting me exactly as I am.

This is what Thomas sees.

What he's missing, this Zerrisenheit, is that now I am torn between two worlds and feel as if I don't fully belong in either. I love life with my husband, son, our dogs, our home on a small lake, our business. I love my adopted country, with all its options and opportunities, its beauty and strangeness, and its culture shifting from east to west, north to south. I never needed to be different; only to accept who I was: a German child cradled in the arms of a country where most everyone is from somewhere else.

I also crave time with family in Germany. When I visit, I usually stay for a month or longer, planning most of my time with Papa. We wear trails in the perfectly groomed parks, toss food to the ducks at the Teich, slurp coffee in the afternoons, and share meals. When we aren't together, I shop for fresh food in Tegut, try on clothes in Markthalle, get my hair done at Modern Friseur. My intention is to spend time with my father, yes. But I also want to see if I can reclaim my German-ness. To be the child remembered so vividly. At my core is that German child still.

Yet it isn't that simple.

When I am with my family in Germany, I mentally share joys and frustrations with my son and husband, who continue while I'm gone with the life we've built together. The comfort of our routines. Our familiar habits, words, and idiosyncrasies. After a month in Germany I am not a stranger. Our life picks up where it left off. Like stepping through a door.

When I'm at home in Florida, I have mental conversations with Papa. I reflect on the time we've spent together and revel in the reminders that he's my father: gentle chiding for not wearing socks, or showing up at my rented flat in the misty rain with a large black umbrella to hold over me as we meander through town. Tiny precious moments.

What might have been, had I grown up with all the German-ness intact? How different would I be if I had not struggled with image, with identity? If I had not felt the need to define myself as someone other than I was? We are the sum of our experiences, our perceptions and beliefs, but also our struggles. Am I richer for mine or poorer? Mine created anger and pugnaciousness that always propelled me forward, to prove myself. Are accomplishments worth the inner turmoil?

Here is the truth: I will never know. So why speak with exaggerated fondness of the home I had, or acrimoniously about the one I didn't? Either would be a lie. Home isn't a Christmas card scene: the perfect family gathered in front of a blazing hearth, smiles oozing love. Home is that place within yourself, that core deep inside. Home is that voice that says you're okay, no matter where you are or who awaits your return. Those you love and those who love you are the foundation, the walls, and the roof. Everything else is up to you.

When I was a child, I plucked snails out of Oma's garden. I piled grasses and leaves into an empty shoebox and watched them for hours. I loved that they were able to carry their homes on their backs, to retreat into whenever they felt the need for safety. I thought about how lucky they were. Now I know that their internal organs are also protected by this shell. Without it they cannot live.

I look up from my thoughts now with a start, to find Thomas quietly watching me. I know he wants a response. I decide I won't share. Not today. As much as I love him, today I don't want his professional assessment or his cousinly advice. At least for a few minutes or hours or days I want to feel the equanimity he sees. I want to keep building my home. I'm not there yet.

PART 3
ACCEPTANCE

"There is something wonderfully bold and liberating about saying yes to our entire imperfect and messy life."
Tara Brach

The Boys of War

Bad Nauheim
June 2019

I feel ill today, definitely jet-lagged. Dizzy, nauseous, dazed. I arrived yesterday morning on the overnight Lufthansa flight and insisted on spending the day at Father's to catch up. My body crashed around 8:00 p.m., and now I'm paying for the marathon. I'm staying at another vacation rental in the upper part of town. A week here with Papa, a drive to the Tower for a week, time with cousin Michael in Neustadt and then back here again for a week before the flight home. Another month in this country I'm reclaiming. Or perhaps it's reclaiming me.

Outside and straight up from a large casement window in the living area sits a bird on a roof gutter. I hear him but I have yet to see him. He began at first light, around 4:30, calling out in a shrill and drawn-out peep. His persistence is impressive and scary. I expect to see his body plummet past the window, exhausted and starved. I can only assume it is a he looking for a mate, to fulfill the reason he lives. To procreate. To have a family. I understand; I've left my husband and son in Florida again for a month to spend time with my German family.

And family we are slowly becoming. Papa, Anni, and I will be meeting Michael, Bettina, and Niklas for an evening meal later this week. With each visit, we have spent some time together, going out to dinner or lunch. We've also enjoyed a few al fresco meals at Michael's villa, about fifteen minutes away in the next town. His backyard is long and deep, flush with fruit trees, groupings of flowers, and a small greenhouse for spring seedlings. A comfortable patio replete with an impressive grill sits close to the villa. And what a grill-meister my brother is. He can create a perfect steak or succulent skewered shrimp. Michael and I chat in both languages. He seems at ease. I'm grateful; he has added instead of replaced. Really, he has no choice. Pictures don't lie, and one in particular shows the three of us—Papa, Michael, and me—sitting in a row: our features and facial expressions leave no doubt we belong together.

After piling pillows on my head to drown out my feathered tormentor, I drag my sorry body out of bed and under a shower. I'm expected at my father's house. We are going somewhere for *Mittagessen* at a special place Anni has picked out. A brisk walk down to their flat revives me some, but I can't think about food without wanting to retch.

Anni drives us to a place fittingly called House by the Lake. Set back in a deep forest, the rustic inn offers a path to a serene and perfectly round lake. I'm able to force down most of an omelet and guzzle three tall glasses of water. I may have simply been dehydrated. Father watches me as I painstakingly chew my food, then asks me about chewing gum, which Germans fittingly call *Kaugummi.* I look at him, puzzled. What exactly does he want to know?

Father says he found it interesting that when American soldiers were captured, they immediately and frantically emptied their pockets of watches, rings, money, cigarettes, and chewing gum—they always seemed to carry gum.

I shrug. "Maybe gum helped pass the time."

He gives me an impatient look.

"No, why did they always hand everything over?"

"Oh. Well, because the Germans were known to take whatever they wanted. The soldiers didn't want to be physically ransacked. Didn't want to be manhandled." I raise my left eyebrow, as in I'm joking, but not really.

"No, no. We had strict orders. It was against rules to take personal items. Maybe the SS did that, but not any of the regular units."

I look down at my food for a couple of beats.

"Well, maybe the regular units weren't allowed to ransack so that the SS could get it all." Another raised eyebrow.

Papa looks thoughtful, then sighs loudly.

Since I had this crack in a door that he prefers to keep closed, I ask him if he took Pervitin while on the front. Pervitin was an early methamphetamine, a stimulant that Hitler purportedly supplied as regular rations to his troops. The drug is touted to have been behind the success of the Blitzkriege as well as the long marches into Russia. A unit can survive on little sleep and less food. Much has been written on the subject and of Hitler's personal drug use, which escalated along with the war.

Father shakes his head adamantly.

"No, only the Luftwaffe, the Air Force, took pills. So they could fly long distances. But Goering was crazy and took drugs. Goering was the head of the Luftwaffe. He met Hitler in prison, you know. In 1923, after the Beer Hall Putsch. He helped Hitler write *Mein Kampf*. And became his right-hand man."

He nods, as if this explains everything. I sit and think again about the prolific propaganda machine Hitler executed so skillfully. Understandably, it's a delicate subject around any German citizen. I have more questions, but Anni asks our server for the check, and we begin to gather our things for the ride back to their flat.

•

Now it is late afternoon. Papa and I are settled comfortably in recliners in the living room as he launches into the story of how he was captured in Normandy in 1944. During the invasion, his legs were hit by shrapnel. Hauled to a makeshift German hospital, he lay recuperating with others in his platoon. Rousted by medics telling him that the Americans are coming, he and a few others attempted to hide by jumping into a large trash bin. They hunkered, shook, and prayed as they listened to bullets pinging off their hiding place.

"The lid opened, and we saw faces looking in. We were commanded to come out. I'll never forget looking up at those tall Americans with guns pointed at us. Oh, how our legs shook!"

My father was seventeen.

They were herded into the back of a large military transport vehicle, *crammed in butt cheek to butt cheek.* On the long ride, one of the guards offered him an American cigarette. It was strong and made him sick. But with this small act of kindness my father held out hope that he and the other young soldiers would be spared death. I asked him how his legs managed to heal. He shook his head, grinned, and stated that being a POW healed him. He either had to work or get whacked.

My father was temporarily held at a makeshift POW camp. Metal fences and barbed wire had been thrown together, divided into holding pens. Like cattle before a slaughter. No shelter. No food or water for days. It rained incessantly, and the puddles offered some water. Soldiers died daily. They stayed where they lay, becoming mounds in the mud. It was bitterly cold.

Finally, on the first day of warm sunshine, a small group of American soldiers sauntered up to the fence with plates of food: sunny-side up eggs, fresh bread, crisply fried potatoes. They paraded along the fence line casually, plates held out at nose level. After a couple of turns, they faced the salivating prisoners and slowly, excruciatingly, dumped the food on the ground, out of reach, and walked away.

Bleak memories for Papa. For me, his images contrast with my own: bodies piled in boxcars and in trenches; starving dark-haired and brown-eyed children; lines of the very young and the very old marching into "showers;" a smokestack spewing the smell of death into the skies day and night. Did my father know what those soldiers had seen in the concentration camps?

Ultimately, it was food that saved him. Farms in Germany and the previously occupied countries lay fallow with no labor to work the fields. Much of Europe was starving. Father was sent to work under a Kriegshilfe, or War Aid, program. For the next two years he plowed fields, planted crops, and milked cows in Belgium. He had a warm bed and plenty to eat. His warden family treated him kindly.

He pulls out a photo album to show me a picture. My incredibly young Papa sits on a milking stool. Dressed in overalls, a cap jauntily pushed off his forehead, his hands work the udders of a large cow that stares calmly off into the distance. Other photos show him years later, after his release. He's a dapper young man dressed well and riding an impressive motorcycle. Next to him stands his old warden. They are arm in arm in front of the farmhouse door.

" I was very lucky."

Papa says this solemnly. My heart lurches. Had he not been wounded, and ultimately captured, he likely would have been another war casualty. When Hitler began his ill-fated push into Stalingrad in the winter of 1943, boys my father's age and younger were sent to the front lines. Those who did not freeze or starve to death became cannon fodder. Or prisoners that did not survive.

According to Papa, the POW camps in Russia were a nightmare. Especially Stalingrad where his brother was interred. He tells me that out of 90,000 German prisoners, only 6,000 came home. His brother Karl did not. Captured as part of the 6th German Army in 1943, the family received word from the German Red Cross that Karl had been shot while trying to escape.

My father shakes his head.

"They said that about all the prisoners they killed. My younger brother Erwin was also fighting at Normandy in 1944, but I didn't know this at the time. He was killed in action."

"We were only boys," he reminds me, and gets up to pull a DVD out of yet another carefully catalogued cabinet. The video begins with aged men sitting at a long table. As the camera pans out, we see what appear to be high school students interviewing them. As they answer questions, the video cuts to grainy black and white: the interviewees as young boys, working as flak helpers in the Luftwaffe. Some of them were only twelve years old. One tells us that his uniform trousers had to be wrapped around twice and fastened with a safety pin. He laughs and points out that it was the first time he had worn long pants; he had only been in the shorts of boyhood.

What strikes me most is the innocence I see in the faces of these children. The posture of their gangly bodies. The veterans speak of the excitement they felt as members of the Hitler Jugend, the HJ. They were thrilled to learn war maneuvers. They rode on rafts, eased up to land, and slipped into the water to crawl ashore. It was a big day for them when they were taught to load and fire the flak guns used to shoot down enemy aircraft.

"We did not feel any remorse. I thought about the enemy flying in to bomb our towns, our homes, and I had no qualms about helping to shoot them down. To kill them."

As we sit side by side, I glance at Papa's face and see a resigned sadness. Sadness that he had been a part of this unconscionable deception. I think about the shrewdness of Hitler's careful and patient brainwashing of the country. After he took over leadership in 1934 following the death of the ineffectual von Hindenburg, all his actions were orchestrated to lead up to war. Especially frightening was his conditioning of the youth. By the time war began, every young boy had learned to fight, kill, and swear total allegiance to the Führer.

The song that became the official national anthem in 1933 was named after its author, Horst Wessel, who penned the lyrics in 1929 while a leader for the SA in Berlin at the age of twenty-two. A student and bohemian, he died in a brawl in his Berlin flat in 1930. It was publicly stated that he was shot in an altercation with communist provocateurs. Wessel was declared a martyr. His marching song, the *Horst Wessel Lied,* was played at all official Nazi functions. It was mandatory to give the Sieg Heil salute anytime the song played. It was also played at all HJ functions.

(*Die Fahne Hoch* … or Raise the Flag High)

Raise the flag! The ranks tightly closed!
The SA marches with calm, steady step.
Comrades shot by the Red Front and reactionaries
March in spirit within our ranks.

Clear the streets for the brown battalions,
Clear the streets for the storm division!

Millions are looking upon the swastika full of hope.
The day of freedom and of bread dawns!

For the last time, the call to arms is sounded!
For the fight, we all stand prepared!
Already Hitler's banners fly over all streets.
The time of bondage will last but a little while now!

Raise the flag! The ranks tightly closed!
The SA march with quiet, steady step.
Comrades shot by the Red Front and reactionaries,
March in spirit within our ranks.

The HJ uniform consisted of a brown cotton shirt with breast pockets, a long neckerchief, and either shorts or trousers in black. The early SA uniform also consisted of a dark tan or brown shirt, often with pants that look like riding breeches tucked into knee-high boots. An easy transition. Eventually, uniforms based on rank were adopted, accent colors signifying rank, although the basic ensemble color stayed the same. By the time war began, every boy over the age of ten was mandated to belong to the HJ.

On June 24, 1943, an armored division was created which consisted entirely of boys under the age of eighteen: 12th SS Panzer Division, Hitlerjugend. It was the brainchild of Artur Axmann, the official leader of the HJ at that time. That winter, Germany had sustained huge losses which included the fall of the 6th Army at Stalingrad, and then in May, the loss of its last African strongholds. Axmann posited to Heinrich Himmler that an infusion of energy and fearlessness was desperately needed. Youth was needed. Hitler approved the plan in February and by September over 16,000 recruits—many of them younger than seventeen—were undergoing intensive training. They were ideologically pure. They swore to die for the Führer.

•

The afternoon sun slants into the room, and I become aware that the video has stopped. We are sitting in silence, deep in our thoughts. Papa turns to me. "I have something to show you." He leads me to his office and wakes up his computer, activating the screensaver. Grainy black and white photos begin to scroll. Small groups of young soldiers, standing or sitting with canteens, grin at the camera. In one, my father, looking proud, is flanked by two older, taller boys as he holds up a field telephone.

"I was in charge of field messages. At sixteen! I ran around with the telephone. Usually away from the front lines. I guess I was one of the lucky ones. There was a strong camaraderie among us. We always looked out for each other."

He turns his chair to me, leans over and looks fierce. "I am so thankful I never had to kill anyone."

I'm surprised that he had the photos as a screensaver, remembering how much he wanted to avoid memories of war. He has obviously been reflecting. Before I can ask what changed his mind, he says he has more photos, a special album of his time in the Wehrmacht. On the opening page are his two brothers in their uniforms. Their death notices are underneath. Other pictures are of Papa with his platoon, set up on the sidelines. His sister's husband also died on the front. The family home in Frankfurt was bombed twice. These are the bad memories. Yet, for a moment, they seem to fall away and the same face drawn down by sadness a few minutes ago is now lit up by the bright eyes of a young boy, proud of his skills and loyal to his countrymen. Unaware of the evil.

Papa in Belgium as Kriegshilfe, circa 1946

Sieglinde's Strength

Sulzbach
July 2019

My aunt is in top form today, hands in pockets of her brown Columbia hiking pants. A grin splits her face and causes her scheming blue eyes to disappear. We are standing in the middle of a main road curving from Highway 14 through Albersdorf, a tiny hamlet with no streetlight. The view is more than worth the risk of traffic that may veer around the bend, although Sieglinde isn't worried a bit. She's plotting and God is helping, so no bloody impact today. Besides, we can see clearly for 360 degrees. Rolling hills and farmland envelope us on all sides. All is quiet except for an occasional horse whinny and clink of bridles coming out of the large barn she's admiring. The sweet scents of hay and horse sweat permeate the air.

"This is new! Whew, it's been a while since I was here last, but I don't remember a riding school. What good news! I can't wait to tell Markus about this and let him bring Zoey. She can take her lessons here. This is great, really great." She looks as if she has solved the last piece of a complicated puzzle.

Sieglinde has an empty flat on the top floor of her large home. Recently renovated with light wood floors and bright cabinetry, it's ready for a tenant. The townhouse originally was the home of Sieglinde's in-laws, built out with private flats on each of four floors. Sieglinde and her husband Schorsh moved into one of the flats after they married; her in-laws remained in another. My aunt tells me in a hushed voice—as if she couldn't believe it herself—that they all managed to live together for over thirty years. After Schorsh's mother passed, Sieglinde took care of his father. The father had never been a gentle man and did his best to break her confident spirit early on. He struck out several times with his fists.

"I sat myself down afterwards and asked God what I should do. But I knew: respect your elders, always. I began to think about the differences in the way men like him, especially those of his generation, react to things. I thought about the major differences between men and women, how they deal differently with the same situations. And I figured out how to respond to him in ways that stifled his anger. I kept myself humble, yet unaffected by his attitude. Slowly, it shifted and we were able to get along."

Sieglinde hopes that Markus will move into the new flat. He is the son who now is single again, sharing custody of his seven-year-old daughter. Currently, he, his ex-wife, and Zoey live in apartments in a suburb of Nurnberg about thirty minutes away. Sieglinde thinks it would be ideal if Markus moved back home, both for her and for him. He hasn't agreed. She keeps looking for ways to entice him.

An airline pilot for thirty-one years, Markus has been grounded since 2012 with extreme blood toxicity symptoms he maintains were caused by jet engine "bleed air." He told me that when we fly, recirculated air is pulled through the engine compressor before being pumped through the pressurized climate control into the cabin. In theory the system works fine. That is, unless the engine seals begin to break down and the air picks up toxic oil fumes as it circulates through the engine. For most of us, our livers are able to filter the toxins out of our organs. Markus maintains that much of jet lag is this process of cleansing. But if someone has a compromised immune system, or an underlying condition, the toxins can build up instead of being expelled. Articles have surfaced online regarding debilitating illnesses of pilots and flight attendants. Some have died.

Markus explained that he and his brothers have a genetic deficiency. They lack certain enzymes for the liver to function properly. What I translate into a methylation deficiency. This allowed the toxins to build up in his system over years. He now spends his time battling his employer, cleansing his vital organs on the Gerson Therapy, and living an extreme organic lifestyle. Devised by Max B. Gerson, a German-born physician in the early 1900s, the therapy consists of juicing, consuming specific raw and cooked vegetables, supplements, and coffee enemas. There are testimonies from people who claim to have been healed of cancer. Markus believes it saved his life. The cost of his illness has been tremendous. Always athletic, strong, and outgoing, he found himself housebound, unable to focus, exhausted. It took years to return to a normal day.

Until recently, his employer paid his full salary while refusing to acknowledge his illness had anything to do with flying. Now he has returned his crisp navy-blue pilot's suit and striped tie. He has also filed a lawsuit. Markus wants to own a health and wellness clinic one day, but can't see his small hometown as a viable location.

Sieglinde will just have to wait this one out. When she bangs her fist on the table and shares what her wants are, I remind her about the firm belief she has in prayer, so get back to it. She nods and looks chastised. Beginning with the revelation from her aunt when she was eight years old, Sieglinde has prayed for guidance in everything. Her Heavenly Father has always been the template for her good life and the foundation of her identity. Yet, the need to know her biological father stayed intrinsic. She needed to know what he looked like. Who he was. The anger she carried for him mounted until the day she visited his gravesite. The hours ticked by as she cried out her pain until there was nothing left. Then she thanked God for giving her the chance to forgive him.

•

We drove here so Sieglinde could show me her husband's family homestead, or where it used to be several generations ago. The land was once a farm with a garden plot, cows and chickens, a plow horse or two and fields of grain waving sleepily. The farm is now gone and a prim stucco two-story home sits here. Schorsh passed away two years ago from colon cancer. He was eighty-eight and had been in good health otherwise. Cousin Michael attended his funeral and told me that Sieglinde sang songs amidst laughter and tears, sending her beloved husband off to his eternal home.

The Fenzels and the Renners are especially entwined. My great-grandmother, the first Uroma who died after a lingering illness, was born a Fenzel. It turns out that Schorsh was a cousin to Sieglinde. She met him when she visited his parents with her aunt Susanne. She says she immediately fell in love.

"It didn't matter that he was ten years older than me. When I told my mother I wanted to marry him, she tried to talk me out of it. I was barely seventeen, he was twenty-six. She asked me why a pretty girl like me would fall in love with such an ugly man. But to me he was beautiful. He had God in him, like I did. And I knew God wanted me to be with him; I asked!"

Schorsh was born with an orofacial cleft in 1929. From first recorded history, a child born with orofacial abnormalities was looked upon with horror and fear. The devil was often mentioned. Sometimes the child was taken into the wilderness and left to die. Today, a cleft lip can be seen on pre-natal ultrasounds and parents get counseling to plan ahead for surgery. A team works with parents to provide feeding and care counseling. Stigma can be avoided, and the child's speech develops normally. But in 1929, the knowledge and skills were not quite there. Especially in a small town in Bavaria.

Little Schorsh's father was devastated when he laid eyes on his newborn son. A devout Christian, he felt God was punishing him by giving him a child he considered a physical abomination. He sat, head in hand for hours and prayed to God to tell him what sin he had committed to deserve this. While he was thus occupied, the baby lay in a hospital bed. Nurses tended to his needs, but his parents were told it would be best for all if they left him to the care of hospital staff. The baby lay day after day, for almost a year, fed and changed but mostly untouched. While his mother cried in anguish, his father paced and prayed. After several surgeries, he was sent home. To a father who never looked at him without revulsion. When a brother was born a few years later and died in infancy, his father cried in anger that God had taken the good child and left him with the evil one.

When Mom, Jackie, and I made our trip in 1983, it was the first time I met my uncle as an adult. His scar was noticeable, and his speech was impaired, although with focus he was understandable. I found him to be quiet and unassuming, comfortable enough in his skin. His deep faith was what people remarked most about, not his physical appearance. As he aged, his white hair, ruddy complexion, and eyes often downcast in prayer reminded me of a sage. His eyes were kind. At family meals, he insisted on many minutes of worship and singing. I remember sitting at the table, delicious scents wafting into my twitching nostrils while Uncle Schorsh, eyes tightly closed, intoned words of praise and gratitude to his Father, feeling, like Sieglinde, that God was the only true father he ever had.

My uncle believed in the healing power of prayer. One afternoon we were visiting, and I found myself with a whopping headache. I asked for ibuprofen. Instead, Uncle Schorsh prayed over me for long minutes, asking occasionally if the headache was gone. I finally said yes (although it wasn't, it was worse) and escaped from the parlor into the cheerful kitchen.

For my aunt, God is lightness and love and blue sky. But for her husband, that same sky was tainted black and resounded with claps of thunder and spears of lightning. God was there to punish those who failed in his commands and whose faith veered in a wrong direction. His doctrine meant no dancing, no dating, no sports, no, no, no … It was one of solemnity and strict adherence to his interpretation of the commandments in the Bible. The only lightness came from music as long as the words praised God. Life was difficult for his intelligent, lively children. W*e were considered religious freaks.* My aunt and uncle devoted themselves to helping folks in the community. Their lives included prayer retreats and long hikes in the beautiful Franconian Jura, camping in the Altmuhl Valley, and a simple way of life.

I can't help but think of the unknown genetics from Sieglinde's biological father. How did they contribute to the traits of Sieglinde's children? They are like her in looks, intelligence, and strength. And have led what would be considered successful lives: Thomas the doctor, Markus the pilot, and Stefan the entrepreneur turned organic farmer. The oldest child, Ruth, was a happy wife and mother when she died in her late twenties from a complication in a routine surgical procedure. Sieglinde's faith was shaken, but again prayer allowed her to heal.

The photo of Sieglinde's father that hangs in her office does not give up its secrets, at least not to me. More than once we stood in front of it, staring intently. My aunt craned her neck to put her profile close to it and demanded to know if I see a resemblance.

"Well, what do you think? Do we look anything alike? Look closely!"

I did see a similarity in the structure of the eyes, the length of the face. But her delicate features are a far cry from the impressive nose and firm set of the lips so prominent in her father's face. The little bit of information she has about him came from his grandson and was hard-won and final. Everything else is guesswork. Mostly she's thankful to have found out where his grave was. It allowed her the closure she needed.

Since Schorsh's death, the boys stay in close touch with their mother. Stefan checks in mornings and Markus sends her a *sleep well* text in the evenings. Thomas calls frequently. All visit with their young children. They share meals in the long cozy kitchen, or spend lazy afternoons in my aunt's peaceful garden, hanging from a rope swing. All three have built their lives elsewhere, but Sieglinde holds out hope that Markus will move back home.

The riding school may be an enticement, she thinks, as she gleefully shares her thoughts. Excitement and a sixteen-ounce bottle of water send her darting into a copse of bushes and trees to pee, while I stand there envious of her boldness. I'll wait until we get to the restaurant Sieglinde has in mind for traditional bratwurst and sauerkraut, with a large lager to wash everything down. As we head out of town, she points to a two-story yellow stucco house on a curve. "I think a distant relative still lives there."

Underpinnings

The Tower
Sulzbach
July 2019

I loved coming to the Tower as a child. The foundation of my childhood has deep roots here. Shivering with excitement, I felt I had stepped onto the pages of Grimm's Fairy Tales. They came vividly to life as I lay on a straw tick mattress in the Tower's top room at night. Aside from the home I shared with Oma, the rest of early childhood images are from here.

I am staying at the Tower again, for two weeks, to hang out with Aunt Sieglinde. Also with Gabi, who spent hours with me last summer helping to investigate the Tower history and the story behind the belt. She's sympathetic to my need to understand our family history. She knows the story of me ringing my father's doorbell and being met with open arms. She knows Oma's story, and her role in helping Hitler populate his vision.

She knows my story now, of being an outlander in two countries. Unlike my own fragmented childhood, Gabi has lived here her entire life, as have most folks in town. Her sister owns a small shop on the main street in town that combines specialty liquor sales with a travel agency. Gabi works there part-time and knows everyone in town. She loves working the street booth during city festivals, serving shots of home-made liquor and bantering with townspeople she's known always, along with tourists who become new friends.

Chic in jeans and a white blouse, Gabi yoo-hoos from the landing outside the open front door. After a quick hug, I lock up and we pass through the creaky front gate to begin our stroll down the narrow cobblestone road called Obere Gasse, or Upper Alley. Two-story apartment buildings line both sides and cast shade for much of the day. Bright flowers and deep greenery stand at each street-level doorway. They give the old stone buildings additional charm. Each one houses several flats, which are individually owned. Gabi hollers "Gruss Gott" to a man in a white undershirt hanging out of a window, then stops to chat with a stout elderly woman who is sweeping her front walk wearing a crisp white apron over her matronly dress and thick stockings. The lyrical Bavarian dialect, with its magnificent rolling Rs, is strong and almost sounds like a foreign language.

We get partway down the street when Gabi stops to point at water gushing from a spring beneath one of the buildings into a small rectangular pool back underground. The spring's fresh water flows on to Rosenbach, a small brook which meanders along the town wall behind the Tower. Gabi tells me that many years ago the women who lived on the street would bring their clothes here to wash.

An image comes to mind, and I'm slammed into stillness as it dawns on me this may be the washerei I remember from my childhood. I've always been adamant that it was located behind the wall of the Tower. A hazy vision of a large place where Uroma Anna did her washing and where I scampered around to collect loose buttons. The shirts and pants were dunked into the freezing water, rubbed vigorously with soap on a thick wooden railing, and then rinsed in fresh water. I also remember a lot of whacking to knock much of the water off before the clothes were wrung out and hauled home in a wicker basket. In the summer, a clothesline outside was fine. In the winter, the half-frozen garments were typically hung in attics, while women sat in front of their fireplaces or wood-burning stoves to thaw their red, raw hands. I imagine Uroma Anna was delighted when she finally got a washing machine.

Now I ask Gabi if she remembers a wooden railing here before the aluminum one. She shrugs. "Could be, probably was at one time." I tell her about my vision, that I remember a much bigger place. She grins and quips that I was also much smaller at the time.

As we approach the end of the street, a row of *Schrebergärten* appear on the right side. Gabi points to one and tells me it used to belong to my great-grandparents. Again, an image flashes. A grubby child running through a garden, picking nubby raspberries and plump red Johannisbeeren. Her fingers drip with scarlet juices. She squats between the rows of lettuce, her boots covered in thick black mud as she bends over to peer underneath the leaves for snails.

I stand riveted at the gate and try desperately to pull up more images, but it's not memory, only imagination. It's impossible to "see" Uroma Anna as she bends over in her cotton house dress and apron to pluck carrots out of the rich loamy soil, or to "see" Uropa as he sits on the bench in the shade, clouds of sweet pipe tobacco drifting into the air. An image of a little girl keeps intruding. She sits in the dark soil to savor the warm smell of sunshine that wafts off the blackened wood hut. This, I think, is memory. But was I here or was I in the garden on Kantstrasse; Oma's garden? I pull myself back to the present and turn to see Gabi watching me patiently. As though she knows my thoughts. A tiny smile plays at the corners of her mouth.

What must my family think? What preconceptions does Gabi have of me? Rumors and suppositions exist as pinpricks in my family's shroud of reticence, unexpectedly surfacing at odd moments. Somewhere at some time, or multiple times, I've been referred to as Susi's accidental child who was adopted by an American Army officer. Who lived in what some may consider exotic locations such as Hawaii and Japan. Are they thankful their lives have been secure and predictable, knowing exactly who and what constitutes that elusive necessity we refer to as home? Not doubting their memories. Or am I foolish to assume that they have made conscious choices to stay close to where they were born? Perhaps they wished they too could have been whisked away to live in other parts of the world. But I doubt it. That feeling rushes back at me, a bubble of anxiety sitting in an empty spot, about to burst. That damn yearning.

•

Gabi nods at me. "Let's go on up to the Literature Archive. They currently have an exhibition I think you'll like."

We turn and walk uphill into town on a street with shops and a large auto garage. Literally straight uphill. Sulzbach sits on massive rocks of limestone; everything is pretty much up and down. Halfway, I stop and exclaim about something—nothing really—in a shop window, to catch a breath. Living in Florida doesn't prepare one for the hills here. We continue and come out on Rosenberger Strasse next to Ortmanns. Across the street catty-corner is the Literaturhaus Oberpfalz, a four-story, white stucco historical building. Ten steps bring us to the heavy timber door. We enter a cool interior.

Two lower floors hold a permanent exhibition and the main purpose of this grand building: literary development after the end of WWII, predominantly in the 1950s and 1960s with a focus on the *Gruppe* 47. Group 47 was an informal association of writers that originated with German war prisoners held in the United States. Their purpose was to reestablish broken traditions of German literature. Concerned that the proliferous propaganda of war had corrupted the language of German writers, members adopted a sparse, realistic style in an attempt to reclaim validity. Life-sized black and white photos of the Gruppe in tuxedos and top hats hang starkly against white walls. Their last meeting was in 1967.

The group's initial political focus relaxed as time went on. Writing styles shifted. Literary prestige rose. Gunter Grass, a German prisoner of war from 1944-1946, had a prolific run. He became a member in 1955, published his first poetry in 1956, a play in 1957, and a Nobel Prize winning novel *Die Blechtrommel (The Tin Drum)* in 1959. Another prominent member of the group was the poet, novelist, professor, publisher, and founder of this *Literaturarchiv*, Walter Hollerer. Born here, he worked and lectured in Frankfurt and

Berlin, where he eventually discovered and became enamored with the Beat Generation writers in the United States.

On the third floor, Gabi and I find a special exhibition: German-American Literary Relations from 1958-1968. Here I discover a close friendship between Hollerer and Gregory Corso, who in turn was close to Jack Kerouac and Allen Ginsberg. Letters, postcards, scribbled notations, and other paraphernalia of correspondence between these four are encapsulated and on display. Sound and film recordings loop. Glass cases contain magazines and books of the 1960s, covers swirling with bright Pop Art.

Gregory Corso's cursive letters to Hollerer always sign off with *Love, Gregory.* Wordy letters from Hollerer to Ginsberg and back again are typewritten. They are concerned with the publicizing of Corso, the youngest of the Beat Poets. With a jolt, an image comes to me: of Ginsberg in a large hall, first whispering and then shouting. Oh! I tell Gabi I saw Ginsberg perform his ranting *Howl* when I was an English Lit student at the University of South Florida in the early 1980s. I had forgotten until now.

After a few hours, my eyes bulge and burn from absorbing and interpreting. Gabi asks if I've had enough, if I'm tired now, as she did the afternoon we spent hours going through Tower papers and photo albums. It's a perfect time to head back to the Tower, where her car is parked. We're driving to Amberg to meet her middle son, Philip, and have dinner.

First mentioned in documents from 1034, Amberg straddles the meandering Vils River, which we cross on a covered bridge to the Altstadt. After admiring the massive Gothic interior and posing for pictures in front of Basilica St. Martin, we find a cozy table in the open Marktplatz to await Philip's arrival. He lives in a nearby flat, doesn't own a car and makes his way to classes at the Technical Museum of Applied Sciences on a bicycle. He arrives, lanky and cute, and slides into a chair, his hand out to shake mine. From photos I've seen of his father Erich, Philip leans toward the French Huguenot features I've only just heard about.

I had mentioned flippantly to Gabi about everyone in our family having Teutonic blue eyes, when she shook her head. "No, no. Erich had brown eyes and so does my daughter, Susanne. It's the French Huguenot features that came from Erich's mother Kuni."

Ah. That also explains the difference in noses. The Renner family is notorious for passing on a long nose that widens dramatically to the tip. I know it well; it was my nose before I had a bit of work done. Erich ended up with his mother's nose, to pass on to Philip.

After coffee we stroll down a short alley to a Greek restaurant Philip has recommended. We eat and drink for the next three hours. *Gemütlichkeit*. When we finally leave the restaurant around 10:30, we walk a short distance with Philip, who turns off to cut through a small alley to his apartment building. Gabi points to his flat on the top floor. I think how thrilling it would have been when I was in my early twenties to live in a town such as this, high up in a renovated building overlooking it all. To be a student with the sole responsibility of learning in those giddy years before the real world intrudes. Then I remember that it has barely been a year since his father died.

As Gabi and I cross the old, covered bridge and totter over the cobblestones to the car park, I wonder about her resilience. A middle-aged woman alone in a large house, surrounded by memories of family, and a husband who died too soon. Her life seems full. She goes to yoga class weekly, works part-time, and has travel plans to fill up this next year. She knows every nook and cranny of this town and several nearby, including many of the residents. A few days ago, we met a longtime friend of hers on the way to the Franconian Jura for a bit of hiking and stopped at a Wirtshaus for lunch. Considered simple and homey, a Wirtshaus is a tavern that offers local home-cooked meals. Usually family owned, mom, dad, brother, and sister all work together, sustained by repeat hungry locals. Gabi knew them all well, with friendships that reached back to childhood. Something I can only imagine.

"Erich was gone a lot. I learned to make a life for myself. I had friends and hobbies, and our children. Erich was an engineer for Siemens and worked on the high-speed Velaro trains used for intercity travel. He was usually gone during the week. And sometimes he would stay over on a Friday night, hobnobbing with other engineers," she shares when I ask how she's adapted to being alone. "It was okay. We had different interests and for some things we had separate lives. Then we had family and vacations we enjoyed together."

Now I understand the kinship I feel with her. Independence, and a strong self is something we share. But she has a quiet resilience that I don't. I'm the one who's riffing emotions. She's the observer who intuits and remains calm. Gabi is also certain where home is, rooted deep in the soil of Bavaria. With a bit of French influence.

The next morning Gabi and Max the Spitz come over to see me off. While Max explores the smells in the kitchen, Gabi hands me a square package wrapped in red paper entwined with a thin gold ribbon. Inside is a *Max and Moritz* book. I'm surprised and touched. At some point we had talked about my childhood love of books, which included *Bummi* books about a German girl and her wacky adventures. (These were later replaced by the outrageous *Pippi Longstocking*.) I also mentioned that I loved *Max and Moritz, a Story of Seven Boyish Pranks*, stories about two young boys with a wicked bend who prank innocent townspeople and end up baked as two loaves of bread. (Written in rhyming couplets by Wilhelm Busch, it's been said they were the inspiration for The Katzenjammer Kids, an American comic strip.) She went out of her way this morning to pick up a copy for me.

In the Literaturarchiv, Sulzbach

Susi

Journal
2019

The January before her death in 2013, my mother came to Florida to visit me. She was living in Jackie's Colorado mountain home and wanted to get out of the cold and snow for a few weeks. During her visit, we both worked hard to be kind to one another. COPD and emphysema limited her activity. A trip to the grocery store sent her to bed for the afternoon, so we dallied over lunches, sat under the oak trees in the backyard and looked out over the lake. We did not talk about the important things we needed to talk about, such as what was happening in her life when she left her infant daughter behind and took on the world. We had reached a quiet truce. The questions still plaguing me receded in the urgency to spend quality time together.

I had adopted a rescue horse in North Carolina and was taking riding lessons in anticipation of her delivery to Florida. I took Mom with me to the ranch on the day of my lesson and sat her in a spot of sunshine near the fence in the paddock. The ancient mare I was learning to ride on shared her grassy acre with a spirited young gelding.

As I was saddling the mare, the gelding sauntered over to my mother nodding off in her chair. He gently began sniffing her face, her hair, her body. A slow smile spread across Mom's face. She sat perfectly still, at ease and clearly delighted. The sniffing went on for many minutes. When Mom opened her eyes, she was nose to nose with her new friend. She lifted her hand and stroked the gelding's soft muzzle. Later, back home, I exclaimed about the gelding's interest in her and his gentleness as his lips nibbled at her hair. That afternoon, as we cradled cups of hot tea, she told me a story.

To the best of my recollection:

I was about three or four, I guess. We were living together at the time, our small family, before my father was sent away to build garrisons. He swooped me up, put me on his shoulders and off to the stables we went. I ran around in the sweet-smelling barn, small enough to walk under the horses, and stroked their warm bellies with my fat fingers. My father swung me on a horse's back, no saddle, and led me around the paddock. The horses were always calm and gentle with me. He also played a mean harmonica and showed me how to blow into one. I kept practicing and soon I could play a little tune. He loved photography and showed me how to look into the lens and frame a picture. My father called me little Felix. I knew he loved me and was proud of me. And then, he was gone. I missed him so.

Here was a blink into her childhood and the father she loved and felt close to. She may have witnessed the altercation between her parents when Felix discovered his wife pregnant with Sieglinde. She may have heard the screams and begging during the awful beating that Katharina took. Mom never mentioned this time, or the days that followed, her mother locked in the bathroom and Felix a madman standing guard at the door. She would have been six. Perhaps she was in school when it happened. Or perhaps she was home, huddled with her younger sisters in a corner of the hallway, helpless. As we now know, Katharina was able to convince Felix that Sieglinde was his. But when he later found his wife pregnant with Christel, he knew for certain the child was not his. Since these are all revelations Sieglinde shared after Mom's death, I will never have the chance to ask her.

Before he was sent to the frontlines, Felix moved in with another woman in Montabaur. When word came back in 1944 that Felix had died, Mom walked to this woman's house and asked if she could have her father's photography equipment. Instead, she ended up with a photograph of him. He's in his Heeren uniform, cigarette in his left gloved hand as he squints into the camera. He looks relaxed, leaning onto a balustrade bordered by a trim hedge that outlines a spacious lawn. An official-looking building sits in the background. We have no information where or when this photo was taken. Except for the wedding portrait, it is the only photo we have of him.

My mother seemed to suffer deeply. The nightmares that plagued her kept her pain alive and saturated her years with sadness and anxiety. But she never spoke of the war horrors she must have seen, or the pain of a family in so much turmoil. So now I can begin to understand how a mother can leave her "accidental" infant behind. The need to escape the memories. Of never wanting to be a Putzfrau in a small town, living a small life and doing what she had always done: clean and take care of others. To have a chance to dance, wear fantastic costumes, be regaled by princes and dignitaries in an exotic country far away, well, this was an opportunity that only came once.

When I was growing up, there were times that Mom put her head in her hands and woefully declared, "I am so stupid." Usually it was a minor thing that set her off, but the self-recrimination would last for hours. She would then launch into the importance of learning, and how I need to be able to "keep my education in my back pocket."

I understand this now to be a reference to the certificate that validated one's skills and was necessary to get a job in Germany. She always regretted that her formal education ended at the age of fourteen. She was needed at home to take care of her five siblings. When the youngest, Hans Herbert, began school, Susi moved to Frankfurt and tried to make a life for herself. But she could only do menial work. And she had her looks. She posed for photographers, hoping to start a modelling career. While working in a restaurant, she met the French woman who would give her a chance to be more than what she was. To get far away from the life she had. And she grabbed that brass ring. But by then I had been born, and we know the rest of the story.

•

In the photo album my mother gave me for my fiftieth birthday is a monochrome of a girl about three years old. She has on a heavy pair of corduroy pants a size too large, a dark wool sweater that rides up high on her waist, and a light-colored knitted cap that ties under her chin with a big bow. But it's not the odd combination of clothes that catches my attention; it is her stance. Her hands are in her front pockets, pushing them out. She is staring at the ground with a lost look. In fact, the whole feeling is one of loss. She makes me think of a Dickensian waif. *Please sir, may I have some more?*

Why does the girl stand like this? Why is the expression on her face one of forlornness? What has just happened, or perhaps has happened over time and brought her to this feeling, here and now? Who took the photo? And why do I not know this girl, this shy one who is saying *don't look at me; I will not look at you.*

It is only recently that I found out my mother had returned after her first contract term ended, perhaps with the intention of creating a life for the two of us. But within a few months she signed a new contract with the same dance troupe and left again. I have no memories of this time. No flash bulb images, no episodic remembrances of my mother's visit and the time we spent together.

The time frame matches up with the waif photo.

To try to understand what I may have been going through, I researched online and found a 2011 article in Psychology Today which discusses *the eyes of love*, or how a child sees herself reflected in her mother's eyes. If she meets with a loving gaze, it lets her know she is loved. According to psychologist Dan Siegal, this is essential to bonding and gives the child a sense of not only herself, but also her place in the world. The child must have this positive eye contact in order for healthy emotional development to occur. Without these mirrored transmissions, the child will likely grow up unable to connect to others. The philosopher William James posited that touch is both the alpha and omega of affection. In moments of deep connection, our brain releases the hormone oxytocin to create an immense sense of well-being, of love. This is the bond between mother and child. The child knows where she belongs. I did not.

•

After his retirement from the Army, my stepfather went to night school and received an accounting degree. He was hired by Florida Gas. When the company merged and became Enron, Ted was relocated to Houston. He and Mom bought a beautiful home in a golf community. When he retired a few years later, they came back to Central Florida.

The home they purchased included a generous yard that butted up to a sandy incline in the back and a view of a small lake in the front. Mom coaxed the sandy soil into producing beautiful flower groupings. The numerous bird baths she erected were quickly dominated by cardinals, Carolina wrens, and mockingbirds, with the occasional blackbird or scrub jay to run the others off. Sandhill cranes strutted through her yard daily on their way to the lake, protesting with a loud bugle call if she was outside. The weather was warm and sunny. Ted played golf. Life was good.

When Ted began to have urinary problems in 2008, he thought it was his prostate. Tests came back inconclusive, and his doctor recommended he get further testing. Instead, he waited. By the time he readdressed the problem it was too late. He had advanced bladder cancer and died in April of 2009. Mom blamed herself for not insisting he continue with testing when it was recommended. Ted hated to go to the doctors and she gave in to his refusal. In the meantime, Mom suffered from osteoarthritis and began taking Hydrocodone for the pain. Eventually she had lumbar surgery and gave up driving. Jackie and her family had already moved to Colorado.

I drove the forty minutes or so back and forth every few days to take Mom shopping and make sure she was doing all right. After her surgery, I stayed with her for a while. It was obvious to all that she couldn't stay by herself. She opted to move in with Jackie. Most of her furniture and her spacious home were sold. The remainder of her belongings were loaded up in a rental truck by Jackie's husband, who drove her and Pippy the cat to their new home in Evergreen.

When she returned to visit me that January, we piled into my Toyota and drove to Florida National Cemetery in Bushnell where Ted is interred. After a stop at the entrance kiosk to get a map, we wound through large green lawns filled with identical simple headstones lined up like sentinels. When we re-located Ted's grave, Mom asked me to give her some time alone. I retreated some distance away and sat under a large live oak. The air was still and warm.

For a long time, Mom knelt at the grave, her head bowed. Then her face collapsed, and angry words tumbled out of her. Alarmed, I began go over, then thought better of it. This was her chance at the closure she needed. After many minutes her tears stopped, she composed her face, and slowly rose, spent. We drove home in silence, and she went straight to her room to rest. That evening she seemed settled; resigned.

After dinner she looked over at me and said fiercely, "He left me alone, all alone. Because he was a stubborn man who tried to be strong. He always had to be strong. I counted on him and now I have to be strong alone. And I don't think I can, anymore."

A few weeks after my mother returned to Colorado that cold January, she developed a problem swallowing food and was admitted into the hospital with aspiration pneumonia. I flew out and stayed for several weeks. Patrick joined us. Every day we gathered in her hospital room, not knowing how long we had with her. She would rally and then regress. But often she was alert and hopeful about going home. One afternoon, Sieglinde phoned. The two sisters stayed on a tearful call. Sieglinde's voice carried into the room as we perched ourselves and kept quiet. After many minutes, my mother agreed to accept the salvation from God that Sieglinde had called to offer.

At the end of February, she left the Lutheran Hospital in Wheat Ridge and moved back into her basement suite. She spent her time reading and fussing over Pippy, her massive Himalayan cat, the only survivor of the four cats she doted on in Florida. As I booked my flight for that summer visit, I resolved to sit in front of her and find answers to the questions I had hoarded for fifty-eight years. Who was my father? What does he look like? What was your life like, and what are your nightmares? What happened to the happy, smiling woman who pulled me onto her lap that Christmas visit so long ago?

Help me to understand you.

To love you.

Please.

•

After I left home to get married at eighteen, I stayed away. Mom and I went years without seeing each other. She was probably relieved. I know I was. That we didn't need to circle around each other, trying to be mother and daughter. I convinced myself that she never loved me. Perhaps she felt I had never loved her.

My mother was always a shell to me, a hard, outer carapace that I couldn't—wouldn't—penetrate. Only since her death have I gotten a sense of the meat and bones and heart and blood and viscera inside the shell. And, most of all, her essence. In order to do her justice, I have to accept her as the person she wanted to be, not as the mother I wanted her to be. As children, we don't think about our parents' lives before they were our parents. We see them as caretakers from whom we eventually break away from, their job being done for better or worse. At some point the roles may become reversed. We become responsible for those who gave us life and kept us alive.

To think of our parents outside of this feels strange and somehow voyeuristic, as if it's not natural, or right, for us to know them any differently. Mostly we feel bonded to our parents. Especially our mothers. They nurtured us with their bodies, endured great pain to bring us into this world, fed us and kept us as comfortable as they were able to. Some are better at this than others, but for the most part maternal instincts kick in when needed and life goes on. The love and caring emanates from this bond.

Sometimes, we can find it in strange ways.

Mom hated to cook. Packaged potato flakes in a yellow soupy mash, khaki-colored beans out of a can, a chunk of gray-tinted meat was a typical meal. All through elementary and middle school, I came home mid-afternoons to find dinner already cooking on the stove. We ate promptly at six, after Ted came home from work. This meant that already processed food had been simmering for several hours.

One afternoon, I came home to an inexplicable transformation: Mom up to her elbows in freshly made dough, the scent of apples, vanilla, and cinnamon thick in the air. Flour dusted the kitchen table, puffs wafting towards escape through the open window. Boxes of golden raisins, miniscule packages of Vanillezucker (authentic, sent from Aunt Christel in Germany) and mounds of tart Granny Smith and sweet Golden Delicious apple slices—almost slivered—sat piled on the edge of the large table awaiting their turn.

I straddled a stool, picked away at the apples and raisins, and marveled at her deft movements. Her gnarly arthritic fingers, strong and sure, massaged the flour and water mixture into a mound. A firm thumb created a volcano crater. Into this she poured a raw beaten egg. Gently, very gently, my mother swirled the dough around and around, further and further, until the egg was absorbed and the mound flattened. She twirled and whirled, a tad more flour, a few droplets more water. When the dough lay glistening, it was ready for the large wooden rolling pin left over from Oma's kitchen. Mom's shoulder muscles contracted again and again as she slammed and rolled, rolled and slammed. When it was over, she rested for a moment, her breath coming out in short bursts.

Satisfied that the perfect oval had the perfect thin-ness, she sprinkled a fine layer of salt overall. With lips pursed, Mom became a painter at her palette. Apple slices became perfectly lined rows; raisins spiraled through the air to land randomly with a plop; freshly grated cinnamon and the precious vanilla sugar rained down on the waiting landscape. I held my breath as she rolled this mountainous pile into a log, the apple slices poking through their almost translucent cover.

And then, my mother, as if she held an infant in her arms, carefully snuggled her creation into a round pyrex bowl. Shavings of creamy butter, a cup of frothy milk, and a fond pat followed before it went into the oven for about an hour.

What came out was a bubbling, heavenly-scented concoction: brown, crispy crust alternated with moist, doughy parts where the log had overlapped. My German mother served this as the evening meal. She proudly presented her masterpiece before positioning it gently in the center of the table. Sitting back, she watched with smug satisfaction as my siblings and I wolfed down the coveted results of her labor. It was only later, after we had our fill, that she would scoop a dollop onto her plate and lift a still-steaming forkful of amber apples and thick doughy goo to her mouth.

This delightful scene became a ritual in the autumn, after the first apple harvest. No recipe was written down; Mom did everything by finger feel and eye measurements. She was proud of her unique concoction, delighted in the process and offered it with open heart. I should have seen the meaning behind this ritual. I should have grabbed onto it with both hands and a full heart. I should have seen the love she was offering, one of the few ways she knew how.

•

A week before I was to fly out on that fateful July to mom-sit, Mom succumbed to pneumonia and was readmitted to the hospital. That night, Jackie held her hand as she took her last rasping breath.

Lance Corporal Felix Fornoff, my grandfather.

I like to think my mother found herself in a meadow, filled with the flowers she loved so much, the warm sun she always craved caressing her skin, the multiple cats she had doted on rubbing against her ankles, and Ted striding towards her with a big smile. I believe she found peace during her golden years. Until Ted's illness overcame him, they seemed content. I believe her choice to marry after all and to give Ted children was her gift for the security and love he gave her. I'm grateful that Ted adopted me. I'm relieved that my mother came back for her wild child, proving she did want me after all.

If only she could have told me.

The Meld

Bad Nauheim
December 2019

I felt as if I had been here in this exact moment before. Jackie and I stand outside the tall apartment building with my father's flat on the top floor. We look up at the bricks that still need to be washed, then down at the name still slightly faded and slanted above the doorbell. I hesitate, transported back three and a half years to the first time I stood here, with nerves galloping and innards turning to mush. A flush of warmth and belonging has now replaced the fear and uncertainty. Inside I hear a door slam, the elevator creak its slow descent. We hear the elevator door slide open, then footsteps continue down the stairs into the basement. No bespectacled older man comes out and asks how he can help us. Not today.

I turn to Jackie, take a deep breath, and push the button that is now so familiar to me. Papa's guttural *Ja* comes out of the intercom. Jackie glances at me and giggles nervously. This is her first time meeting him. The sound of the buzzer signals the building door is now unlocked. I grab the well-worn handle and pull. To the right is a light switch that I flick to illuminate the dark stairway. Our footsteps reverberate off the granite walls as we trot up the three flights. My father is waiting for us in front of his apartment rocking on his heels, bleached-denim eyes shining. He pulls me in for a quick hug and turns to Jackie for a handshake. My sister comes in for a hug instead and they stand there laughing at each other.

"Oh, I like her already." he tells me.

We enter the apartment and Anni comes out of the kitchen, drying her hands on a dishtowel before reaching out to Jackie for a handshake. Jackie tries out her high-school-learned German and the cozy flat comes alive with chatter and laughter as we muddle through the different language barriers. My brother and his family will be here soon. We are having lunch at Tafelspitz, the same restaurant where we first met on that long-ago family day.

And it isn't long before he appears in the still open doorway.

"What's going on here? We heard you down in the lobby. Bettina and Niklas are right behind me."

I introduce my half-sister to my half-brother and get a lump in my throat as I see them together, each one a piece that fits into the whole that is my life. Bettina and Niklas are now outlined in the doorway and we all move into the living room for proper introductions. Anni bustles around Papa. She makes sure he has his hearing aids in as she hands him his navy wool coat and wraps a bright fuchsia wool scarf around his neck. He grabs his wool cap from the coat rack. We head out the door for the three-block walk to the restaurant.

I now know this town almost as well as I know my own, back in Florida. Staying in vacation rentals for weeks at a time has provided a sense of belonging here, a base from which to live the minutiae of daily life. The downtown square with the butcher, the baker, and the floral shop; the small grocery store to grab a few items for supper, or better yet, the bi-weekly farmer's market with its carts of fresh produce and various hand-made sausages.

On those days I grabbed items for a quick but yummy lunch or late dinner I would fix in my flat. Fingerling potatoes with fresh residue of earth still clinging to them, crisp and dark-green asparagus spears, hefty bulbs of garlic and onions, a massive head of buttery kopfsalat, as well as tiny, sweet blueberries or tart currants. All washed down with a glass of crisp Sylvaner or a fruity Grauburgunder wine.

A few times I stayed at a stately old hotel a few streets north of my father's place. The perfect place between trips to visit cousin Michael or the Tower to spend time with Sieglinde, her boys, and with Gabi. But this town always began and ended my visits to the country I was born in. Papa and I have walked these streets and parks for hours. We sat in the large rose garden behind Tafelspitz to chat about everything before choosing which coffee shop to visit that afternoon. We nosed in and out of the small bookstores, sharing our favorites and speculating about the next best seller. When I wasn't with him, I rode around on a rental bike, turning down unknown streets and small trails in a fever of discovery.

Our little group strolls down the sidewalk, past the soccer field and the magnificent Gothic Revival Dankeskirche (Thanksgiving Church) with its seventy foot tower and its floor plan in the shape of a cross. We are a lively bubble of babble as we cross diagonally over two streets and reach the beautiful Art Nouveau courtyard that houses Tafelspitz. The veranda is shut down for the winter. The planters are empty; everything looks a bit forlorn. Tonight, white lights will give the place a festive look, but they are not on in the brilliant afternoon sun.

Serendipity: we are seated at the same long table where my new family had waited to meet me for the first time. As we settle in and slide down the benches to make room for everyone, my mind slips back to that momentous day and compares this comfortable scene with the tense anticipation of that first meeting. Today, the wary look with which my brother greeted me is gone. He's relaxed and chats easily with Jackie. His English and her German meld together. Anni's eyes are soft. Gone is that sad look of reluctant acceptance.

It helps that Jackie is vibrant. Papa catches my eye and nods over at her. "Your sister laughs easily." What I also pick up on is a sense of approval for the family I ended up with. As if he's at peace with the outcome of my life. Emotion wells up and I find myself dangerously close to tears. Fear of rejection had kept me from ringing his bell when Michael first found him in 2009. That, and his initial refusal to see me because the memories were painful. *It was too late.* And yet, on an impulse, we took a chance. How selfish I was! But now as I sit here and revel in this glorious sight, I let go of the voice of guilt that has whispered to me in moments of doubt. I feel like the luckiest girl on earth.

We walk back to the apartment in the already waning December sun. My brother and his family leave us. Hugs and goodbyes take place in the parking lot. We promise to stay in touch until I can come back in summer. (We had no way of knowing then that a global pandemic would make this impossible). Anni takes off to check in on an elderly neighbor who lives alone on the next street. Papa, Jackie, and I settle in the living room. I ask my father to share his photos of Mom with Jackie. She becomes as enthralled as I was, her eyes greedily drinking in the rare sight of our healthy, laughing mother. She pulls up a group of photos she had posted of Mom on Facebook a few days ago on her birthday. Some of them are from her younger days, some taken after she moved to Jackie's in Colorado: on a camping trip, Mom leaning against a rock; Mom and Jackie's girls that was taken after a play, her hair white with one dark streak left over after finally giving up the auburn hair color she used for years. Papa stares. His mouth opens, then closes in a tight line as he shakes his head.

"I would not have recognized her if I had passed her in the street. Ach, ja. I always wished her happiness, even though we couldn't make things work between us. It was difficult for her as a child, helping her mother at home. I met Katharina and liked her. She was a nice woman. I knew she had children from different men, but I couldn't hold that against her. Not then. Those times were hard. I thought Susi was lucky to have her for a mother; she seemed to care a lot for her children. But I knew Susi needed so much more."

The mood in the room has shifted. Each of us sit with our thoughts on this woman. Each of us holds a part of her unique to ourselves. For me she was the person who gave me life and then struggled to give more of herself. For Jackie she was the mother who always hovered, who saw a part of herself in this golden child. For my father she was a dark-haired, flashing-eyed young woman with big dreams. The setting sun makes a weak attempt to slant in through the delicate sheers on the large picture window. A small spot lingers in the middle of the room, shimmers for a moment and is gone. Perhaps Mom's essence has checked in with us.

We sit in the encroaching dusk. Anni returns from her visit to the neighbor, flips on lights. She glances at the photo albums spread out on the beige divan, the same one that my cousin and I perched ourselves so tentatively on three years ago on our first visit. Where Jackie and I now sprawl. Although there's a shift in her eyes, she says nothing. I feel a deep sense of appreciation for this woman who has allowed me to upend her family's life. Who shows me concern and kindness because she loves her husband and I'm a part of him. Could Mom have done the same? I'll never know.

Darkness falls and we say our goodbyes. Papa wants to walk us out, down the three flights of stairs and out to the sidewalk. When I protest that it's dark and cold and he doesn't need to make the trip down, he offers his usual quip: "I just want to make sure you are really leaving." Jackie thinks this is hilarious, but I've heard it enough times to roll my eyes. Anni placates him, says they'll come down to the hotel in the morning to see us off. On the way back to the hotel, Jackie and I stop at one of my favorite cafes for a light dinner and a glass of wine, then call it an early night to pack and rest.

Tomorrow morning Luka Taxi will pull up in front of the hotel at nine to deliver us to Frankfurt Airport for our respective flights. We will get home three days before Christmas. Our families are waiting. My husband John has not met my father. While I've been flying back and forth, he has taken care of our business and our home, allowing me the space and time I need to fully discover Papa and spend time with my German family. I've promised to be home for Christmas. One day soon, I hope my son, husband, and I will fly over as a family.

•

Sulzbach, a week earlier

Here in our maternal hometown, Jackie and I reminisced and speculated on the intriguing story of our family. How many other stories could be out there? How many tragedies, or joys, could be ours if we looked hard and deep enough? Martin Renner, who came from a family of farmers and became part of the Maxhutte steel mill legacy; his son Johann, the young man who wanted more than the mill and was drawn to the allure of power in the SA; our grandmother who got caught up in the fervor that was Nazi Germany and gave herself to create a superior child; our beloved Aunt Sieglinde who continues to astound us with her resilience, her strength, and her joy; our mother Susi who gave us life and nurtured us even when she wanted so much more; and my father, the man who loved my mother and loved me but lived his many years without us, who now has opened his heart and made me whole. We are not unique in tragedy and happenstance. All families have stories with far-reaching consequences. We are fortunate that ours has brought us closer together, created a larger understanding of what it means to be human and decide that it's okay.

In Sieglinde's kitchen one afternoon, my aunt, Jackie, and I pored over Anneliese's old photo album that has brought so much of our history to life. There are a few photos of people who are unknown. Some were taken from a great distance, and we speculate that they could be of young Felix and Katharina, unrecognizable under large hats and long coats. We stare at portraits of life unfurled in the photos: Anneliese in her round top room at the Tower, the background dark as she sits sad-eyed on her bed clutching a doll, surely taken soon after her mother died; Martin in his Maxhutte uniform, standing tall beside his gaunt forced-labor workers at the mill during WWII; Johann in the white shirt and tan shorts of the HJ, legs splayed and arms crossed in a defiant manner; Oma and her girls perfectly groomed and dressed, posing as a statement of motherhood. There is so much here that we will never know because many stories belong to a time in history no one wanted to remember and worked hard to forget. My questions have opened doors that had been tightly closed.

It was at this very kitchen table that my aunt finally heard the confession from her mother back in 1970. Sieglinde had just given birth to Stefan when her mother came for the visit and reluctantly blurted out the truth.

"She spoke very fast, as if she was telling me something dirty. Then she ran out of the room. It was so hard for her to say the words she had kept buried for so long. As you know, I never saw her again. She died within a year."

Sieglinde ushered us into her study to show Jackie the photo of her father that hangs on the wall over her desk. We stood and stared at the strong unsmiling face, trying to get a sense of the man. My aunt's revelation seems so long ago, although it has only been six years. Neither of us can remember the exact café where she blurted out the truth, blindsiding us. When I asked my cousins, they too drew a blank. But we know it happened. Lives changed that night. Through Sieglinde's need to reveal who she was, I felt the need to finally find out who I am and found my father. Knowing our fathers led us to try and understand our mothers. To forgive the choices they made. Because times were what they were, and we have no way of knowing the choices *we* would have made.

We returned to the warmth of the kitchen table. Soon the door flung open, and Markus strode in with his daughter Zoey. Sieglinde's prayers came true. Markus has moved in with her, although not in the new flat upstairs. Instead, renovations in Sieglinde's large flat were underway to provide a private section for Markus, and Zoey during her stays. In the meantime, they share the kitchen and bathrooms and are adjusting to life together.

We walked down to the local Christmas Market. Colorful booths were lined up and vendors sold handmade crafts, spicy gluhwein, and juicy bratwurst ready to burst out of their skins, along with fat, salty pretzels. In a large tent we listened to elementary schoolers with serious faces sing traditional carols while their proud parents and neighbors sang along. The mayor made a short speech and walked among the crowd shaking hands. Jackie introduced herself and explained how she is here from Florida visiting family. They chatted and charmed each other while I snapped photos.

The stars shone bright in a cold sky and folks gathered around huge barrels of glowing fires for warmth. Our group laid claim to one. As everyone laughed and chatted, I looked over to see the outline of our Tower in the near distance, beyond the wall of the brightly lit Sulzbach castle. Heimweh hit me once again as I thought about my maternal family. The many generations who came and went, or who came and stayed. The choices they made influenced by those who came before and the effects on those who came after. I wished that ghosts had visited me the nights I lay awake in that top round room and tried to channel the inner desires of Oma, her brother Johann, great-grandpa Martin and his first wife Katharina. They did not.

Sieglinde's guffaw jolted me out of my reverie. Her head was thrown back, mouth wide open as mirth tumbled out at something that was said. She caught me looking at her and grinned, made her way over to me and linked her arm through mine to pull me aside.

"So, Madlen, you're driving back to your father tomorrow?"

I nod and tell her Jackie and I are spending a couple of days with him before we fly home.

"It's so wonderful that you were able to meet your father and are spending time with him. I wish my story had ended differently. But I'm glad to know who my father was, what he looked like. I desperately needed to know this. So I'm thankful my mother was able to confess to me. I think maybe it helped ease her guilt. You know, I believe she was already very sick when she came to see me in Sulzbach. I believe she needed to clear her conscience. And I forgave her, as I was able to forgive my father that day I cried over his grave. It didn't matter who he was or what he had done. God gave me what I needed."

She hugs herself; rewraps her scarf and adjusts her blue wool cap.

"Let me walk you both back to the Tower before I head home. It's a cold but beautiful night."

I nodded. Looked up at the clear sky filled with stars. We bid good night to the rest of our group. Jackie and I put Sieglinde between us, linked arms, and strolled through town towards the southwestern wall that contains the Tower. I believe the old sentinel still contains family secrets, absorbed by the thick stone walls. Ones I'll probably never know. Nor do I need to. Sieglinde's revelation began an opening of doors that had been tightly closed. Instead of calamity, we experienced a deeper sense of our humanity with all its frailties. She has accepted who she is: a child created for Hitler. Her life has been filled with joy that she has passed on to others. Sieglinde says that God led us right to where he wanted us to be. I'm only thankful that events that began six years ago brought me here, to this time in my life.

Family Epilogue

During the time of my discoveries, I read a heartrending book by Lisa Wingate titled *Before We Were Yours*. It's a novel that interweaves the true story of the notorious Tennessee Children's Home with the fictitious lives of five children stolen from a river shantyboat during the depression and secretly sold to desperate couples unable to have their own. Although the premise is different than my grandmother's, it too deals with loss of identity and the redefinition that became necessary to hide shame and forge a full life. Secrets these children carried to protect themselves and their prominent new families also took a lifetime to reveal.

In the end, one of the characters justified all the emotional turmoil: *the best thing is to know … to know who you is … what you is deep down inside.*

The power of healing came from the revelation of truth.

My journey began with my aunt's revelation. For three years, I tried to ignore it. After all, what possible difference can this knowledge make to any of our lives now? My cousins and I are well into ages that allow for acceptance and lack of histrionics. My grandmother died alone with her shame. We cannot judge the choices she made in times of great upheaval. Or perhaps she did not feel as though they were choices at all, but rather a self-imposed necessity.

On a recent trip, I sat with Aunt Christel on Michael's sprawling patio under a powder-blue summer sky. We slouched, sipped strong coffee, and gazed contently over the acres of ripening vineyards that adjoined the backyard. We pondered Katharina and the choices she made.

Christel shook her perfectly coiffed head, sat up and got serious.

"It was easy for everyone to criticize our mother. How shameful it was to be a thirty-something woman with no husband and six children—three of them born with no man around—but what everyone needs to do is try to walk in her shoes. And remember the times! We have to remember those hard, hard times."

Sometimes, the stories we have carried in our heads, once we tell them to someone, change. The meaning becomes different. The truth, or possibility of truth, changes. I read somewhere that imagination and fiction make up three-quarters of our real lives. I think about my family, my German heritage. I shaded truth growing up as I twitched and wiggled under the mantle of American-ness that I threaded and unthreaded over and over, never able to find a perfect fit. I had my own shame to deal with, my own shadow—a bastard child.

Dominoes. The cascade began in Bavaria many generations ago and touched all in the family, some in small ways and others monumentally. We each have our own story, but they all connect. Fathers and mothers, stepfathers and stepmothers. The power wielded over us and the power we wielded in turn. The effects on us are too numerous to know. Once again, I ask myself how much this all matters. Every family has a secret or two, don't they? The power of love and blood must be greater than our individual heartaches.

I've always held people at bay, knowing that caring for someone gave them the power to inflict pain. I found it safer to remain aloof and keep that careful distance. As a child, solitude served me well. My imaginary friend Mebbie was a voice of reason and a safe companion. We would have long conversations trying to make sense out of what was senseless. I learned to rely on myself, yes, but I also became prickly, self-protective. This journey, discovering my father, my family and the mother I never knew, has taken down my defenses.

Sapere Aude. Centuries ago, Immanuel Kant urged us to dare to know so we can be liberated. Be bold, I hear him say. The truth, when we pursue it with an open heart, will give generously to us. To me, it gave my father. If I had not been in Germany to listen to Sieglinde's story, I may have never ended up on his doorstep. Besides the gift of knowing him, I now know myself more wholly.

It is also through my father's words that I came to understand the person my mother had once been. I wish I had been able to strip away the delusion that anger brings and had open discourse with Mom many years ago. But I didn't. Every time we were together, I felt myself shift away from her, shoulder up in defense. Her crime? Not loving me enough to stay and care for me. Her reasons didn't matter to me. The act did. It was enough to keep her a stranger.

But what if her love was exactly the reason for leaving me? If she couldn't, wouldn't, be able to care for me in her life as waitress and maid, or love my father enough to make us a family, what were her options? I wonder now if there was not a time when she tried to explain. If memory couldn't hang on to the images of the father I so ardently wished for, then perhaps it also doesn't remember Mom's attempted explanations. The anger I carried was powerful and adamant. So was the guilt my mother carried. The two cancelled each other out and left emptiness.

In her later years, my mother lost her power over me. Her health declined. The emphysema and chronic bronchitis took their toll along with the arthritis plaguing her neck and lower back. Finally, empathy replaced anger. We spoke as equals, both of us wizened in years, both of us women with the responsibilities all wives and mothers share. But we never had the important discussions. I was too afraid. Afraid to hear what I had always believed: I was a bastard child, simply tolerated because of my mother's immense sense of responsibility.

If life, if age, gave us wishes along with wisdom, I would spend mine on time. To have another chance to know the woman in those photos—the woman my father knew; that the rest of the world knew. I would spend time wisely, dedicated to conversation and healing. We could hold hands and perhaps ignite a bond that would finally connect us.

I came to understand how stark and unknowable each day was during *those times*, when a nation of decent and hardworking but desperate people were pulled into the extreme ideology, or Weltanschauung, of a single man. My father gave me the power to ask hard questions and perhaps risk losing the support of the family I dearly love. He too wanted to avoid the memories by turning me away on first contact. But he decided to open up to memories and the pain they brought. Hopefully, he found the reward greater than the cost.

And what about my aunts and cousins? Sieglinde's fist slamming the table and declaring the truth be known released the part of her heart that was locked for many years. Knowing who her father was, regardless of what he was, created completeness. As for making the knowledge public, Sieglinde's deep faith has led her to be a witness. As this book was nearing completion, Thomas had a change of heart about putting the story out into the world. His main concern was for his mother's safety, as well as the family's privacy. When he approached Sieglinde, she insisted she wanted this story known, because it may help someone else with a similar one. Her compassion gives her strength.

For Christel, her pragmatic and optimistic outlook on the world merely offered a chance to state her knowledge and shrug, but she too seems lighter. My cousins blew out their frustrations and shock, then settled down to create close bonds. Before we began on our discoveries, it had been years since cousins Thomas and Michael had seen each other. Now they keep in close touch. Jokes about our family with its secrets and facades abound, rendering them harmless.

I know all about facades. I tried on many different faces—not one of them was my own, mostly because I didn't know who I was. With my stepfather in the military, the world changed every few years: a new country, a new home, new schools and schoolmates. By the time I settled into a new locale, it was time to pack up again. Lots of people do this without feeling traumatized. But I also felt a distance with those I lived with, which made for a solitary existence. It's only now, since I've created a solid foundation with my husband, son, and the home we share, that I can lay claim to some sense of stability. But what I've also gained is vulnerability. My walls have been knocked down. Parts of me went to those I love. What they choose to do with them, I have no control over.

Identity. What is it but an acceptance of who we already are? To stop rejecting the parts of ourselves we don't like and grasping for what we think we should be. To reject a mother and grasp for a father. My mother was once considered a beautiful woman, but I hated when people commented that I looked like her. Now people comment that I look like my father and I'm delighted. Can I simply accept that I am part of both? Shame has no place and neither does guilt. I've lived under the weight of both for most of my life. They still hover. But they've been dragged into the light of scrutiny and become transparent.

I believe this has happened with those who share this story with me.

Our quest began with shame, and ended, as so many painful journeys do, with a sense of healing. A discovery of so much more than we—aunts, uncles, cousins and I—set out to understand. Along the way we learned. And this knowledge gave us power. To feel deeply the daily struggle of finding enough food to fill bellies, clothes and shoes that fit and give warmth, wood and coal for heating and cooking. And when we've envisioned that, let's bring in intrinsic human needs for comfort, love, and safety. My grandmother, as a young woman in her thirties, accomplished it all. Not always well, perhaps, but her goals were clear. When I asked Sieglinde to sum up a description of my Oma, she stared off for a few minutes.

"Well, she kept a clean and orderly house. She loved to read. Mutti was strong and acted with courage. Above all, she had a large Herz einer Mutter, a true mother's heart, and wanted the best for all her children. Really, in the end, all she wanted was love and a family."

The Stairstep Girls, in descending order: Katharina, Susi, Erika, Gunda, Sieglinde, Christel, circa 1944

"We tell ourselves stories in order to live...We look for the sermon in the suicide, for the social or moral lesson in the murder of five. We interpret what we see, select the most workable of the multiple choices."
Joan Didion

Appendix 1
Interview with
United States Sergeant Ed Grant

Florida
September 2016

I interviewed ninety-year-old Edward Grant to get an American soldier's view of Germany after the U.S. joined the war in 1941. It was already 1944 before eighteen-year-old Ed finished his basic Army training and became a drill sergeant. A few months later he boarded a transport to Scotland. Much of what Ed told me was repeated in a journal he shared with me, written by another scout in his platoon, nineteen-year-old Hope Clark Waggoner. When Hope died, his family sent the journal to Ed. Both arrived in Glasgow on the RMS Queen Elizabeth, then took a landing craft from Portsmouth England across the channel to Le Havre, France. They were part of the newly formed Mechanized Calvary, on the front lines for Intel (ligence) and Recon (naissance).

Grant was a platoon leader. He and his scouts moved ahead of the rest of the platoon to assess the safety of the surrounding area. They commandeered farmhouses for food and shelter, clearing them of hidden *Jerry* soldiers, holding the owners hostage—at this time very old or very young men and their women—or sometimes expelling them *if they felt so inclined.* Ed shared a story about a family who pleaded to stay. They fed the platoon well and told him about their relatives in Maryland by the name of Baumgartner. A few days later, the team headed back out. They left everything intact.

The squads spent most of their time trying to stay alive and find food. Early on, they found items such as eggs, hidden in the manure piles by the barns, wrapped in oilcloth and tucked in deep. Once they knew this, it was the first place they looked. Often, they also found valuables such as jewelry. (He didn't specify if they took these, and I didn't ask.) For relaxation they played poker and shot craps.

I asked if he felt in constant danger.

"Not really," he replied matter-of-factly. "But in one instance there was a German soldier hiding in the woods near a farm we had commandeered. One night, he climbed up on the roof and dropped a mortar into the chimney which blew out the entire side of the house. Amazingly no one was hurt!"

Once they reached towns, they hunkered down in homes, sometimes for weeks. Here they almost always sent the inhabitants away.

"We would storm in with weapons drawn, check the attics and cellars for hostiles and then give the residents five minutes to get out. They could only take clothes and bare necessities. Everything else our soldiers helped themselves to at will. We didn't feel bad about it at all! We found large warehouses filled with forced laborers from other countries, mostly France and Russia. They were starving and ill; lived in deplorable conditions. On reconnaissance we always reminded ourselves the only good Kraut is a dead Kraut."

The tables had turned on the country that had labelled the Jewish people as sub-human.

Ed said that reasons for hatred multiplied the further they got into the country and went through the concentration camps. The look on his face kept me silent. He didn't mention the condition of the German civilians. I don't know if he wasn't appalled or if he chose not to feel sympathy. Food and supplies were strictly rationed by the end of the war and everything was scarce. Bridges were bombed by both sides to prevent troop and artillery movement, but it also meant no transport for anything, including food from the farms. Whole towns were slowly starving.

It was easy to storm in and take over towns in the spring of 1945. Sometimes German soldiers fought back, but many stepped into the street with hands behind their heads. By April, German soldiers filled the roads walking to the POW camps to surrender. Many were wounded. All were starving.

"There were ten of us in our scouting troop. One day we were marching along from one town to the next when I noticed something was amiss. I counted heads. Now there were eleven of us. A German soldier had infiltrated in the rear." Ed chuckled. "He was only a boy, so we just let him stay with us until we got to the next POW camp."

When the Allies began swarming through Germany, one of the big challenges was to cross the Rhine River which runs from Switzerland to the Netherlands and the Black Sea. It dissects Germany. The allies were thrilled to find the Ludendorff, a railroad bridge in Remagen, still intact; most bridges had been sabotaged by this time. That effort was underway here as the German army loaded it with explosives. Artillery flew back and forth for days as the Allies attempted to buy time in order to cross into the heart of Germany and beyond. The bridge finally collapsed, but by then the Allies had built enough pontoon bridges to transport troops and equipment.

There was no doubt the war was now over. Allied troops infiltrated Bavaria to find Munich was mostly rubble. Platoons would race through the small towns kicking in doors and *blasting damn Jerries from attics, cellars—wherever they could be found. The Air Force would also fly in and strafe a town before the land troops moved in*, writes Hope Waggoner in his journal. He goes on about the forced laborers that *lived in filth;* in one town they found 8,000 in one warehouse, *a pitiful sight … thin and diseased. The roads were filled with these displaced people trying to get home. Many just disappeared.* Too weak to keep going, they lay down and died. These included Czechs, Belgians, Polish, French and Russians. The soldiers moved through towns that were *completely destroyed, cities were burning; Nurnberg was ninety-eight percent destroyed.* His journal ends with this note: after victory had been declared, his troop was housed in a Kotex factory.

What struck me most about the interview and in reading the journal was the unemotional nature of both recountings. Ed's face and voice never gave away any emotions he may have felt. Perhaps because it was many years ago. Perhaps, like my father, he had put away those times. He spoke of the war in impersonal terms. No intense images of starving, diseased and depleted lives intruded into our conversation. No sympathy or expressed horror at what was discovered in the concentration camps. It was also clear that the Germans were not seen as people. They were, simply, the enemy.

Hope's journal also recounted little of the horrors he saw or felt, except what I've already mentioned. The document is extensive, but the tone of it doesn't change much during the year he wrote it. Everything was recorded in a matter-of-fact voice, only changing when he wrote about receiving news from home. Then it became wistful.

Appendix 2
Quartet for the End of Time

On a frigid night in January 1941, four musicians, the composer included, waited to premiere a quartet written in eight movements for the clarinet, cello, violin, and piano. As the musicians blew into their cupped hands and jiggled their legs to keep warm, the venue filled with gaunt men in ragged clothing. They pumped their arms to stay warm as they settled onto unforgiving wooden benches. All save the first row. This was reserved for the guards and their wounded charges, who were placed on meager blankets on the concrete floor in front of them. All became silent as the first strains reached desperate souls in the most unlikely place in the world: a prisoner-of-war camp called Stalag VIIIA in Görlitz, Lower Silesia, a part of Germany closest to the Czech border.

Titled *Quatuor pour la fin du temps*, or Quartet for the End of Time, the piece was written by Oliver Messiaen, a French composer and POW as he hunched over a makeshift desk in a tiny pod of a cell. His German guard, a music lover, supported his composition and was able to make the premier happen. He also gained an early release for the four musicians. The guard purportedly attempted to visit Messiaen after the war but was turned away.

In Messiaen's words: "An upright piano was brought into the camp, very out of tune, the keys of which seemed to stick at random. On this piano I played my *Quatuor pour la fin du Temps*, in front of an audience of 5,000—the most diverse mixture of all classes in society—farmworkers, laborers, intellectuals, career soldiers, doctors and priests. Never have I been listened to with such attention and such understanding."

•

As I'm writing, I'm also listening to the second run through of the fifty-minute piece. Each of the eight movements evokes a different mood, discordant notes trill rampant. As the violin reaches for the stars, the piano vacillates between melancholy and sinister. The first movement is tentative and testing, and by the time the sixth arrives the music is strident and angry. By the seventh, I get a sense of suspense and anticipation, and by the eighth and last, the wait is over. An angel hovers over me while I am left with a sense of reflection and acceptance.

Accounts written of this extraordinary event indicated that everything fell away—the cold, discomfort, pain and despair—and listeners were transported to a place suspended in time and rife with meaning. Look to God, the music seemed to say, look to God. Messiaen dedicated his work *in homage to the Angel of the Apocalypse, who raises his hand towards heaven saying 'There shall be no more time.'*

How fitting then, that it was inspired and written in a place where humanity, even for one hour, was exalted before it once again fell into hell.

legitimate (adj.)

mid-15c., "lawfully begotten, born of parents legally married," from past participle of Old French *legitimer* and directly from Medieval Latin *legitimatus*, past participle of *legitimare* "make lawful, declare to be lawful," from Latin *legitimus* "lawful," originally "fixed by law, in line with the law," from *lex* (genitive *legis*) "law" (see legal). Transferred sense of "genuine, real" is attested from 1550s. Related: *Legitimately*; *legitimateness*. The older adjective in English was *legitime* "lawful, of legitimate birth" (late 14c.), from Old French *legitime*, from Latin *legitimus*.

legitimate (v.)

"establish the legitimacy of, make lawful," 1590s, from Medieval Latin *legitimatus*, past participle of *legitimare* "make lawful" (see legitimate (adj.)). Related: *Legitimated*; *legitimating*.

Afterword

I began this book in 2016, upon my return from Germany after my aunt Sieglinde told her story. In the following four years, I flew back and forth at least twice a year, to spend time with my newly-found father, his family, and my German aunts, uncles, and cousins. Every night I would sit and record any pertinent events and conversations of the day. When I returned, I wrote chapters of that visit. I ended the story after my December 2019 trip with my half-sister Jackie. My father was still healthy, Sieglinde was in top form, and my new family had accepted me. All information had been confirmed or repudiated, and the story ended on a high note. Life was good.

Covid came along and it would be May 2022 before I returned, accompanied by my half-brother Patrick. He had not been back to Germany since our family left when he was barely a year old. It was his first time meeting my father. The following April 2023, my half-sister Jackie and I took a trip; she had met Walter in 2019 and looked forward to spending time with him.

In 2024, my husband and I planned a Viking river cruise on the Danube, beginning in Budapest on March 13th and ending in Regensburg, Germany. My maternal family's hometown, Sulzbach, is less than an hour from Regensburg, so we planned to rent a car, spend two nights in Sulzbach to visit Aunt Sieglinde and then drive to Bad Nauheim where my husband John would finally meet my father.

On March 3, Walter's son Michael emailed me that Papa was in the hospital, nothing drastic, just a bit of trouble breathing. The doctors found some fluid retention, left over from the removal of his spleen. The email was positive, Papa was in good spirits and bored and wanted to go home. I envisioned him talking up the staff in his usual gregarious way.

The next email from my brother Michael turned me inside out; It simply said *I'm sorry. He passed 20 minutes ago in his sleep from a hemorrhagic bleed.*

We moved forward with our plans, but instead of my husband meeting my father, we attended a deeply sad and lovely funeral. The day was bitterly cold. As we filed in a procession to carry his urn to the plane tree sapling he was to be buried under, large clouds rolled in. The non-denominational pastor said a few last words. As the urn was lowered into the ground, a booming thunderclap made everyone jump. Hail began pelting us. And stopped almost immediately. The clouds rolled away and the sun came out.

I felt my father was watching. And he was letting me know everything was okay.

Acknowledgements

First and foremost, thank you to VLP for seeing the value in this story and allowing me to share it with the world. Howard Lovy, your evaluation was spot on and I appreciate your words and recommendation. Jessica Bell and Amie McCracken, the two powerhouses who make VLP what it is, thank you for being who you are. And thank you Sterling Hooker for your astute developmental suggestions.

A huge hug and thank you to my Beta Readers; this product is far from the original you all had to wade through: Mike and Denise Archer, Marty Jones, Liz Curtis, and especially Marcia Krause Bilyk, who took on the task of my first line edits without being asked; you are awesome.

Many thanks to Kase Johnstun, teacher and editor, who stuck with me through my initial editing and insisted the story had legs even when I was ready to give up. And to Allison K. Williams who read the very first "shitty draft" and set me on the right path.

Much appreciation to the publications and editors who loved and published my companion pieces and excerpts: Jen Knox of Unleash Press, Sarah Leamy of Wanderlust Journal, Martha Highers of Under the Sun Magazine, Grande Dame Literary, Lavender Bones Magazine, and TulipTree Publishing.

For fact checking, I relied heavily on the internet (before AI). Many articles came up about Lebensborn, as well as Hochland, one of the first maternity homes for Lebensborn, and Hildegard Trutz, the 18-year-old who told her story of making a baby for Hitler. The

Guardian carried several articles on the Lebensborn program and Lebensspuren, the meeting of a group who had discovered they were created for the Nazi vision and the corresponding book by Georg Lilienthal.

Books I read about Lebensborn that confirmed much of what I had found: *Hitler's Forgotten Children* by Ingrid von Oelhafen and Tim Tate; also *Cradles of the Reich*, historical fiction by Jennifer Coburn. Another book that confirmed facts is *Waltraud, a True Story of Growing Up In Nazi Germany* by Tammy Borden. Two daunting books I delved into: *The Rise and Fall of the Third Reich* by William Shirer, and *Adolf Hitler* by John Toland, both excellent. Sidenote: Hitler's father Alois was illegitimate, born to Maria Anna Schicklgruber and Johann Hiedler. Although Johann eventually married Maria, Alois remained a Schicklgruber. It was many years later that Johann legally accepted Alois as his child. By then Hiedler had been changed to Hitler, and we know the rest of the story. Imagine the Heil Hitler salute as Heil Schicklgruber. History may have changed.

For reading, general support and sideline cheerleading: Nancy Hagel, Juels Marcero, Ava Farrell, Conny Dobbs.

For love and encouragement, and words of truth when I needed them: my sister Jackie Weaver, brother Patrick McKrill, and "other brother" Michael Harth. Also, a big thank you to Jackie for creating the family vine.

To my beloved German family who put up with all my questions and joined me on this journey into the past: Michael and Ivonne, Thomas and Kerstin, Markus, Gabi, Christel, Hans Herbert (RIP) and Irma.

Most of all, my beloved Papa (1926-2024) and his wonderful wife Anni. Equally so, my dear Aunt Sieglinde whose bravery is boundless.

To my husband: Thank you for all you are. Always.

And my son: I love you to the moon and back. Always.

www.ingramcontent.com/pod-product-compliance
Lightning Source LLC
LaVergne TN
LVHW030919080826
845145LV00013B/2963

* 9 7 8 3 9 8 8 3 2 2 2 2 7 *